No Little Places

No Little Places

The Untapped Potential of the Small-Town Church

Ron Klassen and John Koessler

Foreword by Warren W. Wiersbe

Baker Books

A Division of Baker Book House Co
Grand Rapids, Michigan 49516

©1996 by Ron Klassen and John Koessler

Published by Baker Books
a division of Baker Book House Company
P.O. Box 6287, Grand Rapids, MI 49516-6287

Printed in the United States of America

Library of Congress Cataloging-in-Publication Data

Klassen, Ronald, 1957–
    No little places : the untapped potential of the small-town
church / Ronald Klassen and John Koessler.
      p. cm.
    ISBN 0-8010-9014-8 (pbk.)
      1. Small churches. 2. Rural churches. I. Koessler, John, 1953–. II.
Title.
BV637.8.K57 1996
250′.9173′4—dc20   95-47525

For our wives, who treat us like giants
though we have always been in small places,
and our churches, who showed us
that small churches can do big things

In God's sight . . . there are no little places.

Francis Schaeffer

Contents

Foreword

This is an unusual book that's easy to enjoy but difficult to classify.

It's an entertaining book. You'll chuckle a lot and occasionally wipe a tear or two from your eyes.

It's an educational book. You'll learn a lot about small-town America and the changes occurring in American society today. Some of these trends are exciting and encouraging; some of them are frightening. All of them present opportunities for the church to bear witness to Christ.

But most of all, this is a challenging book, a clarion call to action. If individual believers and local churches don't have a big vision for small-town America, we'll be ignoring the wide open door the Lord has set before us.

Written by two seasoned veterans of ministry in small-town America, *No Little Places* is a heart-to-heart account of cross-cultural evangelism right here in the United States. It's a primer on how to discover a church's potential and build on it. It's a transparent how-to-do-it book that pulls no punches. It reads like another chapter in the Book of Acts or extra verses in Hebrews 11.

There are no "big" preachers or "small" churches. But there is a great and mighty God who is still searching for people to trust him to do the impossible in places where the impossible is all that will work.

Warren W. Wiersbe

Acknowledgments

We owe a debt of gratitude to several key people who helped us with this book:

Eddy Hall, our primary editor, who worked through our manuscript with great skill, who drew more stories out of us than we knew were there, and who did with this book what we could not do ourselves: He blended two authors' writings into one.

Paul Engle, acquisitions editor of professional books at Baker Book House, who saw potential with our original manuscript and patiently guided us through the steps to bring it to print.

Warren Wiersbe, who offered to read our original manuscript, spurred us on from there, and encouraged us when we were almost ready to throw in the towel.

Harold Longnecker and Gary Roseboom, colleagues of Ron and friends of John, who read every word of our original manuscript and offered many valuable suggestions.

Phil Somers and Dan Green, fellow pastors and the other two members of our small group, who monthly asked us how the book was coming along and encouraged us to remain friends through the process. (We have!)

Mike Edwards, public relations director at Dallas Seminary, who provided just the editorial pointers and help we needed.

Introduction

What's So Special about the Small-Town Church?

Our culture idolizes size. The most important executives have the biggest desks in the largest offices. The problem with today's "luxury" cars is that they aren't as big as they used to be. Buying a larger home is a sign that you have "moved up" in the world.

While we might wish it weren't true, if we're honest, we know this attitude has made deep inroads into the church. At a pastor's conference, one of the speakers asked anyone there who pastored a church of one hundred or less to stand. Most of us rose to our feet. Yet the conference speakers were all pastors serving in congregations of thousands. I (John) sat down feeling that if I were as good as they were, I would be pastoring a large church too.

Shortly afterward I caught myself apologizing for the size of my church. When introduced, I would say, "I pastor a small church of only seventy-five." I had confused size with significance.

We believe the small church in the small town is important—important to God and important to those it serves and will serve in the future.

One reason many small-town churches have not fulfilled their potential is because their pastors and people have not caught a vision of the possibilities. They may unconsciously feel that only big-city churches can be truly exciting.

Part I of this book struggles with these feelings of insignificance that afflict so many small-church pastors and members, exposes the source of these feelings, and points the way to discovering God's perspective on the significance of the small-town church.

Another reason some small-town churches fall short of their potential is that their pastors and members don't understand the cultural dynamics of the small town. When I (John) accepted the call to become pastor of Valley Chapel in Green Valley, Illinois, I was also accepting an invitation to cross-cultural ministry in a world radically different from the one I knew. Jane and I had lived all our lives in large metropolitan areas. Now we were moving to a town of about seven hundred people. I knew something had changed when we walked down Main Street during our first week in our new home and a wide-eyed girl pointed to us and said, "Mommy, I don't know them."

Much like a missionary to Africa or Asia must learn to relate to a new culture to be effective, Jane and I had to learn to relate to a new culture in Green Valley. Many pastors of small-town churches struggle because they never master the skills of relating across cultures. These skills are critical to fruitful ministry.

Part II of this book introduces the issues of cross-cultural dynamics that are so important to effective pastoral ministry, both in traditional rural towns and in emerging bicultural "rurban" communities.

The other major change we experienced in going to Valley Chapel was the move from a large church to a small church. Most of my life I had belonged to churches of several hundred people. The Sunday school class I taught while in seminary was larger than the church I had come to pastor. I noticed the difference, of course, but hardly thought it significant. After all, I was sure that under my capable leadership, Valley Chapel would soon grow to be the large church I wanted it to be. Besides, I really didn't think size was an issue. Large or small, I figured, the dynamics were the same.

I couldn't have been more wrong.

When I met with the board of elders for the first time, I came armed with the strategies I had learned from those who had pastored large churches and was met with blank stares. The treasurer wanted to know why I thought we should begin using a budget. "We've never used one before," he explained, "and the money has always been there." The chairman wondered why I put evangelism at the top of my list of goals for the next four years. In fact, he wasn't even sure we needed to think four years ahead.

Although the change came slowly, in time I learned to stop judging our church by big-city standards. My greatest teachers in this process were the church's members.

Part III of this book explores the differences between small-church and large-church dynamics and shows how to build on the small church's special strengths in shaping relationships and ministries. The church that follows this approach will never be a pale imitation of a large church, but will uniquely embody in all its gatherings and ministries the small-church sense of intimacy that most large churches can only long for.

If God has called you to pastor a small-town church, this book is for you. It is to encourage you to appreciate more than ever before the importance of the work to which God has called you and to give you and your people practical tools for fulfilling your church's God-given potential.

Your picture will probably never grace the cover of a national magazine. You may never be invited to address your denominational conference. Few may hear or care about the struggles you have faced as you serve Christ in your small town. Do not let that discourage you. There is One who notices. He will bless your efforts and reward your faithfulness.

Whatever your church's size, location, or circumstances, God can do great things there. Because with God, there are no little places.

Part I

Struggling with Significance

1

Five Myths of Ministry Success

On Sunday mornings I stand behind my pulpit looking out over a sea of people so vast I can barely make out who is sitting in the back row. As I preach, a state-of-the-art P.A. system fills the auditorium with my voice. Once the service is over, I retire to my spacious office that can be reached only after passing through a maze of corridors and wading through the secretarial pool.

In my dreams.

In real life, neither of us has ever pastored a megachurch. Chances are, we never will. Yet our fantasies reveal a lot about what, down deep inside, we suspect a successful pastor looks like.

Equating successful ministry with images something like these is probably the rule rather than the exception. In seminary we had one big-name pastor after another paraded in front of us, held up as shining examples. At pastors' conferences, more often than not, the featured speakers are pastors of megachurches.

When a friend was graduating from seminary, he mentioned in his exit interview that he was interested in pastoring a small-town church. The seminary professor who was interviewing him responded, "Why do you want to talk to just fifty people each Sunday? Set your goals higher! Go where the people are!"

So what are we pastors supposed to think? In our professional world, "success" is usually (though sometimes not ad-

19

mittedly) defined by such criteria as the size of the congregation and the impressiveness of the physical facility. When measured by such standards, the pastor of the small church obviously falls short. Is it any wonder then that most of us who pastor small churches have trouble convincing others—or ourselves—that what we are doing is truly significant?

Rejecting the Lies

It's easy to blame our feelings of insignificance on the low esteem in which others hold small-church pastors, but blaming doesn't solve the problem. The root of the problem lies in the fact that we have bought into false standards and expectations. Unconsciously they lead us—not just others—to feel our ministries are not very significant. The power of these myths lies in the fact that we don't acknowledge them. We pretend they're not there, even as we allow them to beat us down and at times distract us from the real work God has called us to do.

The only way out of this trap is to expose these seductive myths and reject them as the lies they are, then begin measuring our ministries by God's standards. What are these debilitating myths?

1. The Numbers Myth: To be significant, a ministry must be big. While attending a Bible conference, I (John) noticed a common pattern in my conversations with people. Their eyes would sparkle with interest as soon as they learned I was a pastor. "That's wonderful!" they would say. Then they would ask, "How big is your church?" As soon as I told them, the conversation would end. Their interest in my ministry depended on the size of my congregation.

As much as I hate that attitude, I have to admit to measuring my ministry by the same standard. When attendance is up, I feel good about what I am doing. When it goes down, I feel like a failure.

2. The Big Place Myth: To be significant, my ministry must be in a big place. When I (Ron) was pastoring in central Nebraska,

I often felt very small. That was partly because our congregation was only sixty, but it was also because the church was way out in the boonies and was anything but glamorous.

Small-church programs rarely will be as impressive as their megachurch counterparts, and small-church facilities usually aren't as elaborate. The potential for numerical growth is not as great in the small town, and even when the church grows, somehow the statistics never look as good as in the city.

3. The Recognition Myth: One measure of the significance of my ministry is how much recognition I receive for it. In 1990 I (Ron) left the pastorate to direct the Rural Home Missionary Association (RHMA), an organization that plants and strengthens small-town churches. I was no longer preaching to my own congregation every Sunday, no longer was a church following my leadership, no longer was I constantly receiving attention and strokes. Instead I was directing a ministry known to only a few people.

I had moved from a town where everyone knew me to a town where almost no one knew me. I found that I felt small and insignificant. Why? I came to the stunning realization that my sense of significance had come largely from the recognition I received for my ministry.

Since early childhood, I had set my heart on becoming a pastor and I had worn that title proudly. My children had been proud I was a pastor, and it hurt when, a few weeks after our move, my five-year-old son asked with obvious disappointment, "Dad, you're not a pastor anymore, are you?" Even my kids felt I was less important.

When I attended church as a layperson, I felt insignificant. I was used to preaching, leading committees and boards, shaping the direction of the church. But when it came time for me to get involved in ministry in our new church, the only opportunity for regular ministry my travel schedule allowed was working with the children's program on Wednesday evenings. Part of my responsibility was to set up chairs and tables and vacuum the floor. Though I had at times done these things as a pastor, it seldom was expected of me. These were things, I felt, that "less important" people did, so doing them made me feel less important.

One day I found myself reluctantly working in the church nursery, tending one- and two-year-olds. *Lord, what are you doing to me?* I cried. *I am gifted to do bigger things but here I am changing dirty diapers!*

My response to taking on menial jobs in the church showed me that my ministry had not been motivated as purely by a desire to serve the Lord as I had thought. Far more than I had known, I had been motivated by the recognition it brought.

4. *The Career Myth: Career advances are signs of a significant ministry.* In the late 1940s and early 1950s, the focus of pastoral ministry in our culture shifted from calling to profession.[1] This change has not been good news for most small congregations who want their pastors to be just that—pastors, not professionals.

When they view pastoral ministry as a profession, many pastors see their first pastorates as "starter churches"—places to learn the ropes before moving on to bigger and better things. They are interested in serving there only as long as needed to "pay their dues" before moving up to the church of their dreams.

When the pastor resigns and accepts a call to a larger church, the congregation usually feels used. They suspect they have only been one—usually the first—rung on the pastor's ladder of professional success. They may feel a little guilty because they cannot afford to pay a competitive salary, yet also frustrated and perhaps even a bit resentful that their pastor refuses to be content with a smaller salary. *Pastors are supposed to serve God,* they reason. *More money shouldn't be a reason to leave.*

To the extent that we are motivated by career advancement, we undermine our own ministries. Rather than giving our whole hearts to serving the people God has called us to, we end up trying to use the people to advance our own careers. By definition, that is exploitation, not ministry.

5. *The Cure-for-Inferiority Myth: If I can just succeed professionally, I'll no longer feel inferior.* Several years of intense ministry had left a fellow pastor nearly exhausted before he came to a freeing insight: "I realized that instead of trying to please Christ, I had been working my tail off trying to earn the approval I never received from my father." While God can heal and wants to heal our hurts from the past, professional success can never fill the hole left by unmet childhood needs.

Sometimes failure in a previous ministry can leave us feeling small, so we redouble our efforts in our present position in hopes of proving our worth. Or perfectionistic tendencies can leave us feeling always inadequate—"I could do better"—no matter how faithfully we serve.

Those who expect professional success to provide the cure for feelings of inferiority, whatever the reasons for fragile self-esteem, will in the end find only disappointment. This is not a need that can be met by "ministry achievements" and "promotions to new levels of ministry."

And, of course, when we are driven by a need to prove our own worth, we sabotage our own ministries, because our work is motivated by what's in it for us rather than out of a desire to serve—and that's not ministry.

Embracing the Truth

But we don't have to measure the effectiveness of our ministries by the false standards of these myths. By rejecting these human standards and replacing them with God's truths, not only in our minds but deep in our hearts, we can experience renewed joy and power in serving wherever God has placed us.

1. *The Quality Principle: God judges my ministry not by its size, but by its quality.* First Corinthians 3:13 says that when

one day God judges our ministries, he will "test the *quality* of each man's work" (emphasis added).

It is true, of course, that the New Testament reports on the numerical growth of the church, but such growth is always attributed to God, not credited to people (e.g., Acts 2:47; 1 Cor. 3:6). Never does Scripture use numerical growth—or the lack of it—to evaluate an individual's ministry. The notion that Peter or Jesus was "successful" when many people responded positively to a sermon or "a failure" when most rejected the message is totally foreign to Scripture. In fact, at times Jesus attracted a multitude, while at other times people deserted him. Did numbers make him a success and lack of numbers make him a failure?

Scripture calls us to servanthood, humility, faithfulness, and right motives. It does not call us to produce big numbers. God expects us to be faithful in carrying out our calls, leaving the results to him.

Today the term *church growth* is used almost exclusively to mean numerical growth. If the numbers go up, the church is growing. If the numbers stay the same, the church is experiencing a "plateau," a buzzword for stagnation. If the numbers are going down, the church must be unhealthy and in a state of decline.

Such thinking is overly simplistic. Numerical growth can take place for wrong reasons. For example, during Jesus' ministry, much of the crowd that followed him was more interested in his miracles than in his message (John 6:26). All of us have seen churches that are getting larger for the wrong reasons. Are such churches really growing?

Plateaus can, of course, be a sign of stagnation. But do they have to be? After a growth spurt, don't churches often benefit from a time of rest and consolidation to adjust to the changes made necessary by growth?

Even numerical decline can at times be a sign of health. The fear that came over those who learned of the deaths of Ananias and Sapphira brought an abrupt stop to the rapid growth of the Jerusalem church and may have scared away some of the less committed (Acts 5:13). When Jesus spoke more openly than before about the cost of discipleship, many of his followers left (John 6:66).

A healthier understanding of growth will focus on the *quality* of the life of the church more than on quantity. Are the members growing in spiritual maturity? Are they developing and using their spiritual gifts? Are they reaching out to more people with the gospel? These are the kinds of criteria a church should use to measure whether it is experiencing healthy growth. Obviously, these are not as quantifiable as numerical growth. A spurt in morning worship attendance can easily be charted on a graph, but how do we measure spiritual maturity? How do we know if people are discovering their spiritual gifts or growing in their ability to share the gospel with others?

One way is to ask. From time to time conduct a churchwide survey asking members to evaluate themselves in each of these areas. Not only can the survey ask members what they are already doing, it can also ask what they would like to be doing. At Valley Chapel, one such survey revealed that 59 percent of the members wanted to continue in their present areas of ministry, 8 percent wanted to change to an area where they felt more qualified, and 20 percent wanted to develop ministry skills in an area where they did not yet feel qualified.

Growth in evangelism should not be measured by the number of converts a church wins each year, but by the number of opportunities it provides for others to hear the gospel. Evaluation should also measure the church's efforts to equip its members for evangelism.

Although the church's commitment to world missions can be measured in dollars and cents, money is not the only indicator. How many times did members pray for the church's missionaries or send them letters? How many members visited mission fields in the previous year?

Growth in spiritual maturity may seem the hardest aspect of church life to measure, but that is partially because we tend to forget that spirituality has practical implications. The Scriptures describe spiritual maturity in behavioral terms: "A student is not above his teacher, but everyone who is fully trained will be like his teacher" (Luke 6:40).

One way a church can measure its spiritual development is to set behavioral objectives for itself. One year the missions department at Valley Chapel set a goal of seeing 10 percent of the congregation's families praying for world missions on a regular basis. That same year one of the objectives of the Sunday school department was to see its young people showing practical concern for the elderly in the congregation by writing to them.

Small-town pastor Ken Vetters writes of the time he tested his congregation following a study of poverty in America by asking a family from a nearby town to pose as transients. The family knocked on the church's back door during a potluck supper and asked for help. Members invited the family in, fed them, and asked them to stay for the program. "I could hardly contain my smile," Vetters explains, "as I opened the program by telling the group that they had already been given a test on the past three months' study material."[2]

Because many of the nonnumerical aspects of church growth are observable, they are also measurable. Along with its numerical goals, a church can set qualitative goals and define how and when they will be measured.

2. The No-Little-Places Principle: Wherever God has called me to minister is an important place. Does being in a small place mean your ministry will be small? When it came time for God to send his Son into the world, he bypassed the city of Jerusalem for the small town of Bethlehem.

John the Baptist's pulpit was out in the desert, in the middle of nowhere (you may be in a place like that). Clearly his "church-growth strategy" would not connect with many today. Yet because of God's sovereign plan, his ministry there touched a lot of lives.

Do you suppose Paul, who was gifted to minister to the masses, ever wondered if God made a mistake by letting him stay holed up in prison cells year after year? Paul tells us in Philippians 1:12–13 that his imprisonment actually helped to spread the gospel.

John Bunyan's greatest ministry too was in prison, when he wrote *Pilgrim's Progress.* Do you even know what Bunyan did when he was not in prison? Jim Elliot's life has had worldwide impact, but he never filled a city stadium. His passion was to take the gospel to an obscure tribe in South America. We admire missionaries who serve in tiny villages halfway around the world. We don't question the significance of their work when it takes them years to develop a small congregation. Is a similar ministry in a small town in North America any less important?

Conventional wisdom tells us that we can have a bigger impact in a city of five hundred thousand than in a city of five hundred. In reality, though, living in a larger city seldom means larger influence. How many of those five hundred thousand people can you relate to?

In the city you pay for an ad in the local paper but wonder if anyone pays attention to it; in a small town your church frequently gets written up in the paper. In a large city when a pastor speaks out on an issue, few even know he spoke; in a small town, when a pastor speaks out, the community listens.

Strategies that say we should go to urban areas because more people are there may need to be rethought. True, there may be a million people within a twenty-mile radius, but the statistic that counts is how many lives we are able to touch. Unless you have the gifts of a Charles Spurgeon or a Harry Ironside, you probably will not relate to any more people in the city than you would in a small town. In fact, a pastor of a church of one hundred in a town of five hundred will probably have more impact on the community than will a pastor of a church of one hundred in a town of five hundred thousand.

Dr. Warren Wiersbe often says, "In the eyes of God there are no small churches, nor are there big preachers." How much God can use you has nothing to do with whether he sends you to a large metropolis, a small town, or a prison cell. It depends on your faithfulness and, even more, on his sovereignty.

Francis Schaeffer, whose ministry was centered in a remote place in Switzerland, wrote:

> No where more than in America are Christians caught up in the twentieth-century syndrome of size. Size will show success. If I am consecrated, there will necessarily be large quantities of people, dollars, etc. This is not so. Not only does God not say that size and spiritual power go together, but he even reverses this (especially in the teaching of Jesus) and tells us to be deliberately careful not to choose a place too big for us.
>
> We all tend to emphasize big works and big places, but all such emphasis is of the flesh. To think in such terms is simply to hearken back to the old, unconverted, egoist, self-centered *me.*[3]

3. The Glory-of-God Principle: God calls me to seek his glory, not mine. That is, I am to serve in a way that inspires others to think more highly of God, not in a manner to make them think more highly of me.

In Jeremiah 45:5 God challenges Jeremiah's scribe, Baruch: "Should you then seek great things for yourself? Seek them not." Am I, like Baruch, trying to build my own ecclesiastical kingdom? If I crave the recognition of my peers, who am I really trying to please?

Do I want to be a star or a servant? Stars seek the spotlight; servants are willing to work for a lifetime in obscurity. They are missionaries laboring in places unknown, people working in inner-city ministries, pastors serving in small churches. Servants don't need the spotlight. They are genuinely working for the Lord.

Jesus, who knew both obscurity and popular acclaim, warned, "Woe to you when all men speak well of you, for that is how their fathers treated the false prophets" (Luke 6:26). If left unchecked, a craving for recognition will blind me to the dangers that accompany success and pave the way for serious failure.

Jesus, who never sought his own glory, but only the glory of the Father who sent him, summarizes in one sentence how we are to seek God's glory: "I have brought you glory on earth by completing the work you gave me to do" (John 17:4).

How can I bring God glory? There's only one way: I must do the work he gave me to do.

4. *The Vocation Principle: I am to approach my ministry as a calling, not as a career.* When we first considered moving to rural Nebraska, my greatest concern was that I might be lost out there. I wondered if anyone would ever find me again. As far as I was concerned, it was on the edge of the world on the way to nowhere. I was afraid that if I moved there, my career would be headed in the same direction. Finally, I had to answer the bottom line question: *Do I want to serve the Lord or do I want to serve my ego?*

I sometimes hear there are more seminary graduates than pastoral positions, that the market is flooded with too many pastors. It may be crowded under the spotlight, but there is always room in the shadows for those willing to be servants. Small-town churches have a great need for good pastors today.

Could it be that there are plenty of pastors around, but not enough who are willing to serve in obscure places? Pastors in small towns must be willing to serve quietly, with little fanfare.

Until we put behind us the motives of career advancement—and even professional survival—and give ourselves fully to obeying God and serving the people he has called us to serve, we are not truly serving God, we're serving ourselves.

5. *The Unconditional Love Principle: God loves me because he is love, not because of anything I do for him.* I (Ron) have found liberation in a fundamental truth: I am significant to God, not because of my accomplishments, but simply because he loves me as his child. This means his love for me does not increase as my accomplishments increase. No matter where I serve in the future or to what degree I excel, God can never love me more than he does right now.

David Roper writes:

> Jesus knew, and He teaches us to know, that our self-identity doesn't arise from what we do but from what we are—fully accepted and beloved children of God.

Once after Jesus' disciples returned from a mission and excitedly reported their success, He countered with the mild rebuke: "Do not rejoice that the spirits submit to you, but rejoice that your names are written in heaven" (Luke 10:20). The disciples felt good about themselves because they had done well. It was far better, Jesus observed, to get one's joy from the knowledge that we're special to God. . . .

The Father's words at Jesus' baptism are significant: "You are my Son, whom I love; with you I am well pleased" (Mark 1:11). What had Jesus done? . . . He hadn't yet preached a sermon, delivered a sinner, or done any of His so-called "mighty deeds." He had, in fact, done nothing we normally associate with greatness.

He was pleasing to the Father merely because He was God's beloved Son. That's all.

And what's true of Him is true of us as well.[4]

Liberated by God's unconditional love and acceptance, I can quit striving for a ministry where I try to earn more of God's admiration and be content where I am.

A Dream Church?

For quite some time, I (John) was restless, wishing God would let me move to a larger church. In time, though, as I will describe more fully in the next chapter, I came to truly believe that God had placed me where he felt I could be most useful. Once I accepted that, I noticed an amazing thing happening: God was making my dreams come true right where I was.

If our dreams are human fantasies based on the world's myths of success, God can help us let go of them and build our ministries on eternal truths. But if our dreams are God-given dreams, he can make them come true wherever we are.

2

In Search of Greener Pastorates

When Bethel Church in suburban Detroit contacted me (John) about being their pastor, Jane and I both thought our dreams had come true. Several things made Bethel seem more appealing than Valley Chapel.

First of all, it was just a few miles from the neighborhood where I had grown up. We had many friends there, and Jane's mother still lived in the area and was excited about having her grandchildren nearby. Accepting the call would mean we could finally go home.

It would also give me the chance to be a senior pastor. I had been chomping at the bit to try my hand in a multistaffed church. With a congregation nearly four times as large as Valley Chapel, Bethel seemed to promise limitless possibilities for ministry. The building was big too. With its classrooms, library, and offices, it looked like a castle compared to the little storefront in which we had been worshiping.

After my initial meeting with the pulpit committee, I felt sure they would ask me to candidate. I was also certain that if I did candidate, the congregation would invite me to become their pastor. Everything looked good.

While Valley Chapel was in the middle of a building program, I didn't expect that to be a problem since the building was scheduled to be completed months before I would have to leave. But on that score I proved wrong. As construction proceeded, we ran into one delay and then another, and by the time I was finally invited to candidate, Valley Chapel's building still wasn't finished.

It soon became clear that if I went to Bethel, my last Sunday at Valley Chapel would coincide with our first service in the new building. Now I was in a quandary. How could I say yes? Our church had worked so hard to see its dream become a reality that it seemed heartless to turn what should be a day of rejoicing into a day of mourning. But how could I say no? I wanted to be a senior pastor and I wanted to go home.

When Bethel asked me to candidate I said yes, fully convinced God wanted me to move. A week before we were to candidate, however, I kept a monthly lunch appointment with Dan and Mike, two fellow pastors, and explained my dilemma to them. To my surprise, instead of being excited about my prospect, they had misgivings about the timing. They confronted me, questioning whether it was God's will for me to take the church.

I left the restaurant feeling hurt and angry. "They're just jealous," I told myself. But deep inside I knew they were only voicing the very questions I had been trying to ignore.

Jane and I talked for hours about the pros and cons of leaving, focusing mostly on the pros. Finally, a few days before we were to go to Detroit to candidate, Jane looked at me after one of our discussions and said, "We're not supposed to go to Bethel, are we?"

"No, I don't think we are," I agreed dejectedly.

"What are we going to do?" she asked.

Not only was I to candidate the following Sunday, but Bethel had planned a large dinner in our honor for Saturday night. It was too late to call it off.

"I think we have to go through with the visit," I said. "Maybe they'll make it easy on us and not ask me to be their pastor."

Secretly I hoped my sense of God's will would change during the visit and I would feel the liberty to say yes. Sure enough, my feelings about the decision did change. But not in the way I expected.

Under other circumstances I would have been thrilled by what Jane and I saw as we pulled into the church's large parking lot the Saturday of the dinner, but that night we groaned. Emblazoned in huge letters on the church's sign was the greeting: "WELCOME JOHN KOESSLER."

The people were friendly and the meetings went well. But as I answered the congregation's questions, a strange thing happened. I kept thinking of my little congregation back in Green Valley. I thought about the sacrifices they had made to complete the building and their excitement about its potential for expanded ministry. I thought about their enthusiasm and the vision many of them had for reaching the community. When I looked out over the congregation at Bethel, I saw the smiles of my church family in Green Valley, and an amazing thought struck me: What I already had was better than what I was being offered.

It wasn't that I saw anything wrong with Bethel; it was a fine congregation with a full program. Yet somehow comparing the two congregations helped me realize how good Valley Chapel truly was and how good its people had been to me. That was when I had my change of heart. We began the weekend knowing we had to stay at Valley Chapel. We ended it knowing we also wanted to.

At the end of my fifth year at Valley Chapel we decided to put the résumés away, settle in for the long haul, and learn to enjoy the gift God had given us. In the months that followed I was more aware of my congregation's strengths and less impatient with its shortcomings. When I described the church to colleagues, I heard myself being more affirming.

I knew a change had taken place when at the post office one spring morning one of our members said, "The Lord's been working in your life lately, hasn't he?"

"Yes, he has," I answered. "What have you noticed?"

"Oh, I don't know," she said, "you seem to have more freedom in your ministry these days. Somehow before it always seemed like we weren't quite good enough for you."

33

She was right. Although Jane and I still missed our family and friends, we no longer dreamed of moving back to the Detroit area. To be sure, we still sometimes felt frustrated with small-town life, but most of the time we felt privileged to serve the congregation of Valley Chapel and excited about its future. I told one of my colleagues, "I've come to realize that I like being here. I like what I am doing and I like where I am doing it."

Why We Are Glad We Stayed

Why did we stay? Initially it was a matter of integrity. We didn't feel it was fair to the church to leave in a way that would spoil Valley Chapel's joy in completing its biggest project ever. It was also a question of obedience. We stayed because we didn't feel a sense of liberty from the Lord permitting us to go.

But I now believe God had another purpose in keeping us in Green Valley: so we could see some of the fruit of our labor. If we had left after four years, we would have missed seeing how the congregation's initial pride in completing our building blossomed into a steady confidence toward God that has consistently challenged the church to move out of its comfort zone. We never would have seen Valley Chapel develop its passion for world missions—a passion that has since led several of its members to become personally involved through short-term missions. We would never have known some of the people who are now our closest friends, because they would have come into the church after we left. But most important of all, I doubt that we would have learned the lesson of contentment.

I would like to think that if we had gone to Bethel, my ministry there would have been as fruitful as it has been at Valley Chapel. I suspect, though, that we would have grown frustrated and moved on after a few years. It is likely that such a move would have signaled the beginning of a series of short-term pastorates.

What We Learned

Because we stayed at Valley Chapel longer than we had orig-inally planned, I learned several critical lessons.

I learned that it takes about five years to lay the groundwork for an effective ministry in the small church. Our experience was that during our first two years, the church was still getting over its previous pastor. During the third through fifth years it was testing the current pastor. By the sixth year I had finally earned the kind of credibility that creates the potential for sig-nificant change.

I believe our experience is typical. Why does it take so long? Every few years, most small churches experience the emotional equivalent of divorce as they watch their pastors abandon them for more attractive congregations. In time, members come to expect abandonment, and this leads to a loss of trust.

It's not their pastors' integrity the members doubt; it's their pastors' commitment to them. Because they expect the pastors to leave after a few years, the people wonder if they can trust their pastors to look out for the churches' long-term best interests.

Longtime members have seen pastor after pastor sweep in and pressure the congregation to adopt their ideas. After three or four or five years, they move on, leaving the churches to deal with the turmoil caused because they set significant changes in motion but left before seeing them through to completion.

Most psychologists would consider a family whose husband and father abandoned them every four or five years to be seri-ously dysfunctional. Yet in the family-like structure of the small church, such a pattern is considered normal. We pastors have shown far too little concern for how disruptive our professional restlessness is to the churches we serve, perhaps because when considering changing churches, we do not take into account the family nature of the small church.

When a pastor stays longer, though, he can earn his con-gregation's confidence. One elder who through the years had often questioned the wisdom of my suggestions came up to me after a board meeting and said, "You almost always have good ideas." What made the difference? I had been there seven years and had finally earned his trust.

Of those who were hesitant to follow my lead when I first arrived at Valley Chapel nine years ago, some came to trust me; others left the church. Either way the result was a greater freedom to lead. By the time I left, the "old guard" was made up of many I had once considered the "new guard."

I learned that the pressure I felt to succeed had as much to do with self-promotion as with promoting God's kingdom. I was eager to establish the kind of record that would lead to a call to the bigger church I felt I deserved. When obstacles arose or the church did not seem to progress as quickly as I thought it should, some of my impatience was because I feared my future prospects were being threatened.

If my real goal is to fulfill my calling, not to advance my career, I can accomplish it without "moving up the ladder." I used to say I wanted to move to a larger church because I needed a bigger challenge. I came to see that this small community offered plenty of challenges. Indeed, my real problem may have been that I found it too challenging.

How could we meet our expanding ministry demands with a limited pool of workers? How could we reach the alienated youth of our community, many of whom were sexually active and alcohol abusers? How could we minister to the growing population of senior citizens, many of whom lived in near isolation? How could we respond to those whose marriages were crumbling or who were unemployed? There were enough ministry challenges there to last a lifetime.

As an alternative to measuring my own ministry by the standard of numerical results that are so often used as the basis for invitations to larger churches, I have found it helpful to measure myself by the seven qualitative benchmarks Kent and Barbara Hughes list in their book, *Liberating Ministry from the Success Syndrome:*

- Faithfulness to God through obedience and hard work
- Service to God and others
- Love for God
- Genuine faith
- A vital prayer life
- The practice of holiness
- A positive attitude[1]

These standards acknowledge the reality that God is more interested in what he is doing in me than in what he is doing through me. I tend to be most concerned about what I do; God is more concerned about what I am.

I learned how important a support group can be. The turning point in my struggle over whether to accept the call from Bethel came during my monthly lunch with fellow pastors Dan and Mike. Despite my excitement about the church, they were skeptical about the match.

"John," Mike said, "you almost seem as if you are ready to accept any offer, just as long as it takes you out of Green Valley and back to Detroit."

"You guys could be a little more supportive," I complained. His challenge made me angry but they refused to budge.

"Why do you think we get together like this?" Dan asked. "Do you want us to just pat you on the back and say we think it's a good decision?"

I knew he was right. The idea for our monthly lunch had come during the quarterly meeting of a regional pastor's fellowship. As we ate together, we all agreed that the time spent over lunch was the most beneficial part of the meeting.

"Sometimes I think we should just skip the rest of the meeting and spend the entire time at lunch," I said.

"Why don't we?" someone suggested. "Why not meet together over lunch some day and just spend the time talking?"

A month later Dan called and asked if I was still interested. "I feel like I need the friendship of some other pastors to survive in the ministry," he explained. We set the date, chose the restaurant, and began a relationship that still continues today.

Our format is simple. Once a month we eat lunch together, then spend the rest of the time talking and sharing prayer concerns. Then we close by praying for one another. Topics of discussion range from theological issues to marital concerns to our latest frustrations with the flock. At times, one member of the group dominates the discussion if he is struggling with a particular issue. More often we spend equal time sharing.

For a while we tried reading a book about pastoral ministry and using one of its chapters as the focus of our discussion. When that seemed to stifle our meeting, we returned to our original open forum.

This meeting holds a place of priority on our monthly schedules. Each of us keeps the fourth Tuesday of the month clear, making exceptions only for illness or genuine emergencies. We are also committed to confidentiality. Because we know that what is said over lunch will not be shared with others, we feel free to be completely transparent with one another.

This kind of trust takes time to develop. When members are added, the group dynamics inevitably change, often resulting in a temporary loss of intimacy. When Mike relocated to North Dakota, two new members joined our group. It took about a year for me to adjust to the group's new personality.

Over the years, the perspective of this group has helped me through many rough spots and been a regular source of encouragement and insight. I have often wondered whether I would still be in pastoral ministry if I had not had their support.

The Danger of a Roving Eye

It was shocking for me to realize that I had a roving eye. Although I had committed to one relationship, I always seemed to be on the lookout for another that would be more attractive. It's not that the one I had was so bad. It's just that it was, well, so average. I wanted a relationship that was more exciting. One where I felt more appreciated.

I am not talking here about my marriage, but my ministry. One day while flipping through the ministry want ads in a Christian magazine, I realized I was professionally profligate. Every so often another church would catch my eye, and I would flirt with it by sending out my résumé. Soon a courtship would ensue, and the thrill of the chase would begin, made all the more exciting by my need to keep the relationship secret from the congregation I was serving.

In time I came to see that it was the chase that enthralled me most. Once a church expressed interest in me, I seemed to lose interest. Eventually I became convinced that my professional restlessness was sparked by many of the same insecurities that drive other pastors into extramarital affairs.

A Key to the Small Church's Future

Why do so many small-town churches never seem to get beyond the survival mode? Certainly there are several factors, but the rapid turnover of pastors in these churches is one of the largest. It is hard to plan for the future if you know that every few years you will be looking for a new pastor.

It seems to be the rule rather than the exception for pastors to view small-town churches as stepping stones on their way to pastoring larger churches. It's not that we want to hurt the churches we serve. We sincerely want to minister while we're there, but we are haunted by the thought that the ideal church, the church of our dreams, lies just over the horizon.

Just for a moment, imagine that it isn't a church we are talking about, but a marriage. What counsel would you offer? I think you would tell the spouse with the roving eye to be more realistic, to recognize that the ideal relationship doesn't exist. You would probably point out that a relationship based solely on what the other party has to offer is self-centered, doomed to disappoint in the end. Most importantly, I suspect you would point to commitment as the ultimate solution.

This does not mean that every pastor who moves to a different church is making a mistake. Eugene Peterson, who has argued forcefully for regarding pastoral ministry as a vocation rather than a profession and feels that twenty-, thirty-, and even forty-year-long pastorates ought to be the norm, points out that staying when it is time to move on can be as damaging as moving when we ought to stay.[2]

It is time, however, for us to take a hard look at how damaging short pastoral tenures have been to the small-town church. If we truly are putting ministry ahead of career, we will seriously consider making longer-term commitments to small-town churches, staying long enough to earn trust and to provide the strong, stable leadership they need to reach out to the community.

This will not be as easy as it sounds. In fact, for most of us it will be a struggle. Career-minded ambition does not die easily or quietly. Well-meaning friends and colleagues will rush to our "aid" and try to resuscitate it for us. But for our own well-being, as well as the church's, we must learn to see things differently.

Developing a long-term commitment to our current congregations will take more than simply wanting to. It will require us to retrain ourselves to evaluate our ministries qualitatively more than quantitatively. And it will probably mean building an effective, ongoing network of support to keep us focused on our callings and to encourage us through those inevitable times of discouragement. We will need to remind ourselves that the best place is not always the biggest or even the most comfortable place. The best place is the place of God's appointment.

If we choose to stay longer and take the steps that make that possible, I believe we will overwhelmingly discover that the grass is not necessarily greener on the other side of the fence. When we commit ourselves to long-term ministry, we will find the best place is this place. The grass will become greener right where we are.

Part II

Bridging the Culture Gap

3

A City Slicker in Ranch Country

I t should have been the high point of my year.

My plate was piled high with turkey and all the trimmings of a Christmas feast. In the semidarkness, as I lifted my glass to drink, it caught the gentle flicker of the hurricane lamp that graced the center of our table. Off to my right the Christmas tree blended the classic elegance of simple white lights reflecting off red satin balls with the country charm of red gingham bows tied to its branches. It was freezing outside, the ground buried beneath ice and snow, but inside, the music of holiday conversation interjected with laughter harmonized with the familiar carols playing in the background to fill the room with an unmistakable warmth.

Yet somehow I didn't feel the Christmas cheer. I (Ron) and my wife Roxy had been planning and working for this moment for months. Our annual Christmas banquet was the biggest event of our church year. It was something we had started since coming to Brewster to pastor a couple of years earlier—a time to not only celebrate Christ's birth together, but also to reach out to those connected with the church through family or friends but who seldom attended.

By the time people had started arriving for the banquet, I was exhausted. I had spent the day moving massive oak pews out of the sanctuary and stacking them in Sunday school rooms, then moving in borrowed folding tables and chairs. But it was more than a physical weariness that kept me from entering into the Christmas spirit. It was also a weariness of spirit.

I looked around the room at the more than one hundred people who had gathered for the evening and thought, "Why am I doing all this? This isn't connecting. It's not working."

My greatest hope for this evening was that it would reach the unchurched men in our community whose wives and children attended our church. They were there all right, but I found that small comfort when I looked around the room at these men and realized most of them hadn't been in the church building since last year's banquet. I had no reason to expect it to be any different this time around.

I had struggled to know how to connect with these people from the moment we first set foot in Brewster. We were from different worlds. I had grown up in a city of nine hundred thousand and gone to seminary in a metropolitan area of three million. The town of Brewster, Nebraska, had twenty-one residents—*after* Roxy and I moved in—and the entire county had a population of just nine hundred.

Before we candidated at Brewster, people warned us it was out in the boonies, but nothing they said prepared us for what we found when we got there. The church was eleven miles out of town. As we left the highway to drive the last mile to the church building, we found ourselves on a single lane sand road. Except for the highway, we would learn, all the roads around Brewster are single-lane sand roads. To reach the church, we had to cross a river on a single-lane, ice-covered bridge—with no guardrails. As our car crept across that bridge for the first time, I had the distinct impression I was leaving behind the world as I knew it and entering a vast unknown.

Indeed I was. Everyone around Brewster was either a rancher or somehow involved in the cattle business. Most had large families. At once we felt like misfits. "Do you really think we would fit in?" we asked. "Around here everyone's lives seem to revolve around cattle and kids. And we don't have any of either."

But that didn't seem to bother them. The only question they had for us was "Will you come?"

Even before I preached the sermon that Sunday morning, I had my answer to that one figured out. I would just make it through the day as best I could, then tell them we weren't interested. It was just too different. It didn't feel at all like home. But God had other plans. Something happened in our hearts that day. Before we left Brewster, he had arranged for us to fall deeply in love with these people. We said yes.

Fresh out of seminary, I was eager to bring strong new leadership to the Brewster church, to generate new excitement, stimulate new growth. And I didn't have to look far to find places to make improvements.

First of all, in hiring me, the church had said it wanted a pastor who would be a strong Bible teacher. It hadn't had that kind of pastor for some time, and I assured it that I would make study my highest priority, that I would religiously devote twenty-plus hours a week to study and sermon preparation.

Second, even on the Sunday I candidated, I saw immediately various ways the Sunday morning service could be made to run more smoothly. There were long lulls in the service, like when the Scripture reader waited until the soloist had returned to her seat before he began his walk to the pulpit. The pianist and song leader hadn't coordinated their music like I was accustomed to in the city churches I'd attended. In fact, most of the service seemed to be conducted with little advance preparation. Yes, there was lots of room for improvement in the worship service.

Third, I began dreaming of ways to fix up the building. The gray paneling in the sanctuary had some bulges in it. Some of the ceiling tiles were broken. The table in the foyer, a rocker in the nursery, a kitchen table—all were hand-me-downs donated by church families. It wouldn't be hard to get new furnishings to replace them.

From the moment we moved to Brewster, I put my whole heart into my work. I put in more than the twenty-plus hours a week in my study I had promised and preached to the very best of my ability. I started calling on those with the strongest musical abilities to provide music more often and called on those with less strong voices less often. I contacted in advance the Scripture readers and musicians for each service and tried to impress on them the importance of practicing so they would do the best job they possibly could. And Roxy and I began quietly making improvements to the building to bring its appearance closer to our expectations.

We did all this and then we watched—watched for signs of new life. We watched for evidence of renewed spiritual growth. We looked for new excitement. We watched for attendance to increase. Perhaps as much as anything, we waited for people to express appreciation for the marked improvements we had brought to the church.

People were polite. They didn't complain about the changes. But for the most part, neither did they seem to see the new ways of doing things as any better than the old ways.

The annual Christmas banquet was one of the improvements I had introduced, and obviously people enjoyed it. But as I sat at my table that night, eating with these people I had come to care so deeply about, it was equally obvious that the banquet was not accomplishing its intended purpose. Nor, for that matter, were most of the other new things I had tried. I just wasn't connecting with these people beyond a superficial level. And I had no idea why.

Then one Sunday morning as the children were singing for the congregation—not anything they had practiced but just one of the songs they had learned in Sunday school—I looked out over the people and was amazed by what I saw. Though the children weren't singing exceptionally well, I saw people smiling and nodding. I would do things to near perfection and receive only polite responses. These children were singing at a level anything but perfect, yet they were getting through. The people loved it.

And that's when I realized what I had been doing. I had been trying to impose my city culture on these ranchers, and it hadn't been working. It wasn't ever going to work. I needed to change my whole approach to pastoring.

I knew almost nothing about the ranching culture of central Nebraska. These people were all experts in it. If I wanted to learn how to minister effectively in Brewster, I was going to have to become their student. I would have to look to them to show me what they and the community would be most receptive to.

Over the next few months, my ministry began to change. The church had inherited a substantial sum of money, and I had mentally gone through the building, room by room, visualizing how I could use that money to renovate the entire facility. Had I been pastoring a suburban church, my plans would have been appropriate, perhaps even crucial to the church's future. But when I began looking at our church through the eyes of the people of Brewster, I realized how totally unimportant it would be to the people of our community for us to renovate the building. It wouldn't attract new people. It wouldn't make anyone more comfortable. It would serve no ministry purpose at all. We continued to maintain the building, of course, and fixed up little things from time to time, but I gave up my fantasy of trying to make our little building look more like a suburban church facility.

I also became more relaxed about our Sunday morning services. Though I had been doing most of the public praying and Scripture reading myself, so it would be done "right," I started asking others to take part more often, and I stopped nagging them to be sure to practice so they could do their parts "well." I stopped being so concerned about carefully outlining each service in advance and began to let things happen more spontaneously— more the way they had done things before I introduced my "improvements." When the service didn't proceed as smoothly as it had in the city churches I'd attended, I no longer let it bother me.

But the most important change of all came in how I used my time. I quit spending so many hours a week hidden away in my study and started spending a lot more time with people. Though I had no particular personal interest in hunting, for the sake of spending time with the men, I learned to hunt. I spent a lot more time hanging out at the local cafe, the place where the ranchers gathered daily to socialize.

In the city, I knew, the last thing in the world people wanted was for their pastor to spend a day with them in the office. I would have just been in their way. But I found that ranchers liked to have me put on my jeans and boots, jump in the pickup with them, ride along in the tractor as they planted corn, or go along to a cattle sale.

When one rancher, who along with his wife had visited our church a time or two, invited me to help work his calves, I jumped at the chance. Not wanting to admit my ignorance, though, I didn't tell him I had never worked calves before.

When I got to the ranch, the rancher assigned me the job of wrestling the young calves into the chute. It sounded easy enough, so I hopped into the pen and went after my first calf. I grabbed it around the middle and tried to move it toward the chute, but the calf was stronger than I was. I wrestled and fought with that calf, but no matter how hard I tried, I couldn't get it into the chute. Before long, I was lying flat on my face in manure. Worst of all, while all this was going on, eight seasoned cowboys were leaning against the fence, enjoying the show.

I knew they were all desperately wanting to howl with laughter, but they somehow restrained themselves. (I have no illusions, though, as to who was laughed about over coffee in our local cafe for the next couple of days.) Then those cowboys showed me what to do. You don't grab a calf around the middle; you put one arm around its neck and use the other hand to grab its tail. The neck wasn't so bad, but I discovered that the tail area is not the cleanest part of a calf.

After spending the better part of a day wrestling several hundred calves, I was bone tired and covered with manure. But I had made some friends, and the rancher who had invited me to help him became a part of our church.

That December when the church presented me with its annual Christmas gift, I was surprised on opening it to find a shotgun. I never would have considered asking for a shotgun for Christmas. I'd never even thought of owning one. But that shotgun today is one of my most prized possessions, because in giving it, the men of the church, some of whom hadn't even been there a year or two earlier, were saying, "Hey, you're one of us."

The eloquent sermons, the highly polished worship services, the picture-perfect building that I thought would bring growth and renewal—I had brought all these expectations with me from my city culture. None of them were important to the people of Brewster. What was important to them was personal relationships, a sense of family within the community and within the church.

As we approached what would be one of our last Christmases in Brewster, one of the young women in the church stood up in a congregational meeting and suggested we have a Christmas Day service at the church. Christmas? When everyone is spending the day with relatives? I didn't think it would work, but I went ahead and scheduled the service anyway.

On Christmas Day, so the handful of people who showed up wouldn't feel like we were rattling around in an empty sanctuary, I pulled a few pews around the piano in a semicircle, then pushed the rest of the pews to the back of the room. But as people started coming, the two rows of pews I'd set up filled quickly, and we had to pull more pews, and minutes later, still more, back up to the front. Rather than staying home with their relatives, people brought their relatives with them. By the time everyone arrived, there were sixty of us gathered around the piano, about the same number we'd have on a typical Sunday morning.

Because I hadn't seen the service as any big deal, I hadn't prepared much. The whole thing was pretty informal and spontaneous. We sang carols, people shared, and I gave a short devotional. Unlike a Sunday morning service where the children had to be still and quiet, the morning had a warm, lighthearted, celebratory feel to it, as though we were one big family gathered around the piano. I had shown up expecting almost nothing. By the end of the morning, I knew I had experienced one of the highlights of my ministry.

My city approach—the Christmas banquet that called for months of planning and exhausting preparations—had brought polite response but no changed lives. Yet an approach reflecting the local culture—informal, laid back, spontaneous, unpolished—had led to an ever-deepening sense of family and steady growth in our church family as men, women, and children committed themselves to God and the church.

I had made, and eventually learned from, one of the mistakes most frequently made in leading the rural church—trying to pastor the rural church as though it were a suburban church. Most seminaries unintentionally contribute to this mistake. The methods and strategies taught in seminaries, with few exceptions, have been developed in the suburban church. They work there. They are often taught as though they will work in any church. But as I had to learn so painfully, many of them don't.

Am I saying that suburban culture is bad and rural culture good? Not at all. What I am saying is that as a city slicker coming to a rural area, I was embarking on cross-cultural ministry. I could not be effective in that ministry until I became a student of the culture in which I had come to minister, until I left behind the ways of doing things that I had brought with me from my previous culture, then learned to minister in ways appropriate to my adopted culture.

Though this insight came slowly and painfully for me, it is nothing new. It is the timeless secret of cross-cultural ministry articulated by Paul more than nineteen hundred years ago: "To the Jews I became like a Jew, to win the Jews. To those under the law I became like one under the law . . . so as to win those under the law" (1 Cor. 9:20). As I learned to become "all things to all people," I began to win some.

But trying to impose suburban culture on the rural church isn't the only serious strategic mistake pastors of small-town churches can make. Another error has already led to the death of hundreds of rural churches and is responsible for the steady decline of thousands more. Unless this error is recognized and corrected, sooner or later most of these congregations will shrivel up and die. The next chapter explains what is afflicting these churches and shows how they can be revitalized.

4

The New Rurban Frontier

Tired of the noise and hubbub of the city, it had been Todd Sullivan's longtime dream to move to a more relaxed, small-town setting. His wife, Jodi, a gynecologist, spent only two days in the office each week, so when Todd's employer let him start doing much of his work from home using computer networking, they knew the chance they had been waiting for had come.

It wasn't hard to convince their two teenage children that relocating to a small town would be a good move—especially once they realized they'd probably make the boys' and girls' high school basketball teams. Adam dreamed of four-wheeling around the countryside, and Allison was excited about smaller school classes that would make it easier to form close friendships.

The Sullivans sold their upper-middle-class home in the city and bought a two-year-old house with a large lot on the edge of Morristown, population twenty-five hundred. It was important to the family, and especially Todd, that they become part of the community, that they not be aloof or considered outsiders. So even though they could have still attended their church in the city (it was just twenty-five minutes away), the family agreed to look for a church in Morristown, a church in which they could be fully involved.

Because of their doctrinal beliefs, Todd and Jodi felt that only one, maybe two, of the six churches in town would suit them. So, a few weeks after their move, on a Sunday morning, the Sullivans visited the church they assumed would become theirs.

The first thing Jodi noticed on entering the sanctuary was the three mismatched colors of paneling on the walls. The family was seated on a worn wooden pew bolted to a scratched green-tile floor, a far cry from the comfortable padded chairs they were used to. While waiting for the service to begin Jodi read through her bulletin. She was surprised at how much the typographical errors and uneven type bothered her. They were so different from the sharp, laser-perfect print she had come to take for granted.

During the service when all the songs were sung from worn hymnals and accompanied by a small organ with little volume, Jodi missed the overhead projector and electronic keyboard their church in the city used. The sermon was long and not particularly interesting, and it lacked the clear life-application they had come to expect. Several times during the sermon Jodi found her mind—and eyes—wandering. How long had it been since someone cleaned the dead bugs out of the light fixtures? How old were those water stains on the ceiling tiles above the platform? Why was there a little ceramic church sitting on the communion table?

Jodi knew how important it was to Todd that their family immerse themselves in the community, so she was dreading having to answer his inevitable question, "Well, what did you think?" She was relieved when, on the way home, Allison asked, "Dad, do we really have to go to this church? I don't know if I could stand it. Why can't we keep going to our church?"

This story doesn't describe just one incident, but is a composite of many such stories we have witnessed or heard from other pastors. No doubt this scene has been reenacted in various forms thousands of times in the past decade. Rural churches, operating in ways that have served them well for many years, are finding they can no longer attract or hold the families now moving into their communities.

Our friend Stan found just such a situation when he became pastor of Sand Creek Community Church.[1] The church had been declining for about eight years, and had fallen from an average attendance of 350 to about 250, even though the population of the area had been growing dramatically.

The leaders of the congregation had a sense that all was not well but they didn't know exactly what was wrong. They were looking to Stan to help them figure it out and correct it.

It didn't take Stan long to identify the reason for the church's decline. The church building was in the middle of a corn field and had always been a "farm" church. Many of the longtime leaders of the congregation were farmers or in farm-related work. The church saw itself as a rural, extended-family church.

But while Sand Creek had continued to operate in the familiar mode of the "country church," the community around the church had been drastically changing. The nearest city had grown rapidly, expanding in the direction of Sand Creek Church, until the church was only five minutes from the edge of town. Within a few miles from the church, older farming communities had become expanding bedroom communities. The farm population of the area was declining, and because it was continuing to operate as a country church, Sand Creek simply wasn't attracting and holding many of the newcomers to the area.

So while the members saw Sand Creek as a country church, from the beginning of his pastorate Stan saw it as a church serving a changing population that included not only farmers, but also a mushrooming population of professionals and the students of two universities.

Over the next few months, Stan initiated a strategic planning process through which he worked with the people of the church to come up with a vision of what the church could be and develop a ministry plan. Throughout this process the people made it clear that they loved their heritage and didn't want to lose the feel that had made the church so special to them. But they also accepted the challenge to extend their ministry to everyone in the community, not just one segment of the population.

The plan was in place within less than a year, and in response to the church's new outreaches, new people started coming, most of them from town and from the nearby bedroom communities. They included young professionals, both singles and couples, and university students.

The transition from being a "farm" church to a bicultural church went smoothly at first, but when more newcomers than expected began coming all at once, some people were shellshocked. Sand Creek had always been a dressy church, but many of the newcomers dressed much more casually. An old farmer who had sat in a certain pew for thirty years might show up one Sunday to find a male college student with long hair and an earring sitting in his spot, excited to be there because he had just discovered Christ.

The new ministry plan led to administrative changes that gave elders and deacons more authority, so the process of change would not be so cumbersome. And though the pace of change still seemed slow to Stan, it was too fast for some others. Some of the newcomers, who were not related to any of the families that had traditionally staffed the ministries of the church, moved into prominent ministry roles even though they hadn't been part of the church for long. That's not the way things had been done before.

The music and worship style of the church changed. The old hymns were joined by contemporary music that appealed more to the younger newcomers, and this became the occasion of considerable conflict. Two cultures were clashing, and Stan had to have many long, patient conversations with people during this time. He prepared a six-page handout based on a citing of almost every reference to music in the Bible as a way of helping people distinguish between their cultural preferences for certain styles of music and issues of right and wrong. He made clear that on such issues, people from each culture had to give a little. "It would not be fair to these college students who are just coming to Christ if they never learned the great hymns of the church," he explained. "These are important to our heritage. But they also need the more contemporary music that speaks to their culture. Both are important."

From the pulpit, Stan focused on the person and work of Christ and emphasized the need for the longtime attender with a rural background and the university student to respect each other's love of Christ. "Just because others show their love for Christ in different ways than you do doesn't mean they love him any less," he explained.

Not everyone liked the changes. Some, who had been satisfied with the country church the way it had been, left once the changes began. But today the two cultures have been successfully blended at Sand Creek. University students and those with rural backgrounds worship side by side and have learned to love and respect one another. The process of learning to embrace those of another culture has not only opened the door to renewed growth in numbers, but it has also produced growth in maturity for those from both cultures.

Trends

Sand Creek is typical of many of the smaller communities in North America that are undergoing enormous change. As Sand Creek's story illustrates, a different kind of community calls for different approaches to ministry. Four trends account for the most significant changes taking place in today's small towns.

Trend #1: The number of people working in agriculture-related fields is declining rapidly. Early in this century, almost every small town in North America was a farm town. In 1920, 30 percent of all Americans were farmers. Today the figure is 1.9 percent.[2] Farm equipment has gotten bigger, much bigger, so that it takes far fewer farmers to run the equipment. For farmers this is not a happy trend. As pastors we have lived with members as they fought against rising farm costs and lower income and grieved with some when they eventually lost their farms.

How can the church respond? In a time when pessimism and discouragement permeate daily life in many small towns, the church needs to be an oasis of support and encouragement. Farmers don't need the church telling them how they could have done things differently to avoid losing their farms. They need a listening ear, a shoulder to cry on. They need a church family that will stand by them in crisis, that will build them up when they are feeling beaten down.

Pastors need to set the tone for this. Because farming today is often a matter of the survival of the fittest, many farmers who don't make it have privately concluded that they aren't worth much since they obviously are not among the "fittest." Pastors need to administer the strong medicine of encouragement to farmers suffering from low self-esteem and depression. You can do this privately through personal contacts and short notes and publicly through upbeat, encouraging services with practical, uplifting sermons.

You might consider a sermon series on starting over. Possible topics could include:

Starting Over as a Christian (a salvation message)
Starting Over after Failure
Starting Over with a New Vocation
Starting Over in the Church

(This final sermon would focus on changes needed in the church due to the community's shift toward a nonfarm culture. More on this later.)

While you are building up others, take care to guard your own mental and emotional well-being. Pessimism is contagious. While farmers struggle with self-image because of the decline of agriculture, the pastor may similarly suffer because of decline in the church. It can help farmer and pastor alike if they recognize that the forces behind the decline may be much bigger than any one farmer or any one pastor.

For example, rather than measuring growth strictly in terms of attendance, compare attendance to the changing population of the community. In one of Ron's pastorates, the church declined by one-fifth while the county population declined by one-third. Even though the church appeared to be in decline, in relation to the size of the community, it was growing.

The greatest challenge facing many small-town churches is avoiding slipping into a survival—or even a maintenance—mentality. A vicious cycle can develop: The church desperately needs new people to keep from dying. To get new people, the church needs to update its facility and launch new ministries. But how can the church with declining attendance do these things? And why do them anyway if the church is going to die in a few years?

One member of a rural church would consistently say at church meetings, "Why should we do such and such? The church will be closed in five years." Obviously, such a mentality will paralyze a church. The pastor went to the church member privately and said, "Listen, if the church is going to close in five years, why waste money and effort now? Let's close it this week." That member never made another negative public comment again. Today that church's facility has been upgraded and its membership is larger and younger.[3]

Counter a survival mentality in your church by encouraging the people to take risks for God. Anticipate ways your church might grow. The pastor just mentioned, after assuming a new pastorate, asked the Sunday school superintendent why there was no high school Sunday school class. He answered, "We don't have any high school kids. When high schoolers start attending, we'll start a class."

The pastor responded by offering a class so youth would have a place to come, and they came. In this and other ways he helped to jar the church out of its survival mentality.[4]

Trend #2: Nonfarm, small-town population is increasing. Although there are fewer farmers, most small towns are growing. During a recent ten-year period,[5] U.S. towns of twenty-five hundred or less in nonurban areas (population centers of less than fifty thousand) grew by 4.9 percent. Twenty-five percent of all Americans live in these towns. This compares to a 2.4 percent increase in urban population during the same time period.[6] In spite of all we hear about urbanization, these statistics show there is actually a greater movement toward small towns than toward the cities.

Trend #3: Small towns are experiencing massive demographic changes. If farm population is decreasing but small-town population is increasing, then who is living in small towns today? Professional white-collar people are moving to small towns, transforming them into bedroom communities. For some, rapid transportation makes this practical. Others are simply locating their offices in small towns. With computer networking and fax machines, many business people today don't need to be in the offices where their employers are located. They can choose where they want to work.[7]

Industry is also rapidly shifting to small towns where they can find more cost-effective work forces. David Heenan, an expert on business trends, calls small towns "the new corporate frontier." The driving force behind corporations moving to the small towns, says Heenan, "is the technologies—fax machines, cellular phones. . . . It gives small towns a chance to participate in the post-industrial economy" in ways they couldn't ten years ago.[8] And so we have Saturn cars being manufactured in small-town Tennessee and Little Debbie's cookies being baked in small-town Arkansas.

Retirees are also revitalizing small towns, according to *U.S.A. Today*, "from the mountains of Appalachia to the deserts of the Southwest, from Idlewild, Michigan, to Sayre, Oklahoma. . . . Experts anticipate a flood beginning in the next decade when the baby boom generation begins to retire."[9] The *Dallas Morning News* echoes that "demographers and sociologists have identified five hundred 'retirement' counties across the United States . . . where growth in the 1980s was . . . nearly double the growth in urban areas."[10]

A new generation of people is arising that is enraptured with the idea of small-town living. The Gallup Organization recently asked Americans in what kind of place they would like to live. Nineteen percent preferred the city, 22 percent a farm, 24 percent a suburb, and 34 percent a small town.[11]

The people choosing small-town life today usually want a quiet town with its wonderful small-town values, but they also want big-city attractions close by.[12] A new word—"rurban"—has been coined to refer to these people who have moved to a rural setting while holding on to their urban cultural mind-set.[13] When these people come to church, they bring their dual culture with them. They expect the church to offer the best of both worlds—an up-to-date educational program, contemporary music, and a modern facility, along with the rural folksiness. If the congregation also includes traditional-thinking rural people with the mind-set of a generation past, the arrival of these rurbanites sets the stage for conflict.

In *Developing Your Small Church's Potential,* Dudley and Walrath explain:

> While local persons may welcome these newcomers at first, if the newcomers push for too much change (in other words, for more change than the locals want), the culturally mixed congregation becomes a stressful congregation. Such congregations face real hazards. Those in which newcomers truly dominate often discover they are losing their appeal to long-standing residents. . . . When such culturally mixed congregations lose their appeal to those who are native to the area and are unable to broaden their appeal sufficiently to include a large number of new persons moving into the area, they can lose heavily. They end up as churches that appeal to *neither* locals nor newcomers . . . stressed as they are between two cultures. . . . Culturally mixed congregations are especially vulnerable to conflict.[14]

This situation is unlikely to go away anytime soon. Rather, it appears that this "rurban" demographic shift will continue at least through the next generation.

What is the church to do? Can this new generation of small-town residents coexist in the same church with traditional small-town residents? The answer is yes. We have seen it happen in many churches. But it calls for unusual wisdom and skill from the leaders, especially the pastors, of these churches.

First, pastors must educate their congregations about the demographic changes taking place in small towns. You can ask your people to wrestle with the question: If we don't change to appeal to newcomers, what will happen to our church? The inevitable answer may not be obvious to them at first: If we continue to operate like a farm church, we will die, because the number of farmers is continuing to decline. About four thousand U.S. churches die each year, many of them in small towns where they appealed to a declining segment of the population. For churches that refuse to change, the mortality rate is 100 percent.

Second, you can help your people see that these changes do not involve compromising truth or changing doctrine, but rather making cultural adjustments to respond to the changing culture. You can point to 1 Corinthians 9:19–23 where Paul clearly says we must adapt to the culture around us to effectively communicate the gospel rather than expecting those around us to adapt to our culture.

You can make clear that the things that need changing don't need to be changed because they are bad. In fact, as a part of making changes, you might want to celebrate the longevity and successes of ministries that have served the church well over the years and pray that the new ways of ministering will serve this generation just as effectively as the old ways have served in the past.

People are more likely to embrace changes if they come up with the ideas themselves than if someone tries to impose them. You can help your congregation come up with creative responses to change by asking well-chosen questions: Have you noticed that fewer young people are coming to our services? What might we be able to do to change that?

Many churches have split over conflicts between new and old when no issues of truth were at stake. You can help your congregation decide: Do we want this to happen to us? Wouldn't we rather live with change, as uncomfortable as that can be at times, than go through a church split?

Third, pastors need to accept the hard fact that the church will probably lose some people no matter how well the conflict between old and new is handled. And sometimes, as much as you would hope otherwise, you will face the question: Would I rather lose those of the old traditional mind-set that is only going to lead to the decline and eventual demise of the church, or would I rather lose the next generation?

But by no means does this mean you should write off your older members. Those over sixty are almost twice as likely to be in church on the average Sunday as those between eighteen and twenty-four. Their financial contributions greatly exceed the average giving of younger members, and their willingness to work creates a stabilizing influence. Many times, even if they are more comfortable with the old ways, they can be helped to see the value of change.

Some time ago an elderly couple was wrestling with changes taking place in their church. They were more comfortable with the old ways and wanted to hang on to them. But it was also important to them that the church be alive and healthy for their two-year-old granddaughter as she grew up.

One day when talking with friends about this tension, suddenly the key issue came into focus for them: *We may have to choose between the past and the future, between clinging to our old ways and having a vital church for our children and grandchildren.* Seen in this light, choosing change became easier for them.

Trend #4: The new generation of small-town residents exhibits a marked decline in spiritual and moral values. A survey by the National Rural Development Institute, an organization that promotes rural living, found that rural children fared worse than their nonrural counterparts in thirty-four out of thirty-nine statistical categories, including immorality, substance abuse, and crime.[15]

While these statistics do not describe every small town—there are many wholesome exceptions—in many small towns an alarming number of young people are sexually active and addicted to alcohol.

The family, once a mainstay of the rural community, is experiencing the same kind of disintegration taking place in urban areas. In fact, the number of single-mother families in nonmetropolitan communities has been increasing at a faster rate than in metropolitan areas.[16]

Before living in small towns, we would have been shocked by these findings but can now confirm them from personal observation. One of us lived in a small town where almost all the fifty high school students were sexually active. Many abused alcohol. Parents gave their teenage children—and sometimes younger children—access to beer in their refrigerators, rationalizing that, like it or not, every teenager will have a vice, and alcohol is a better vice than drugs. The best basketball player in the high school was killed along with a friend in a car accident while playing chicken in a drunken stupor.

Why is this fourth trend happening? Perhaps partly because young people, some recently transplanted from the city, find small-town life boring, with limited options of ways to occupy their time—and alcohol and sex are readily available. But could it also be because many small-town churches have failed to adapt to the changing needs of their communities and because some churches continue to operate much as they did a generation ago, and so have nothing to say to a new generation of small-town residents? Is there a connection between the thousands of rural churches that die each year and increasing immorality among small-town youth?

These four trends broadly describe fundamental changes taking place in many, probably most, small towns in North America. But some or all of them may not be taking place in your town. Studying trends is no substitute for becoming an astute student of your own community and its culture.

For example, the story of the Brewster, Nebraska, church in chapter 3 and the story of the Sand Creek church earlier in this chapter may seem to make almost opposite points. In Brewster, Ron discovered that he was trying to impose changes too quickly, before learning enough about the culture to know what next steps were culturally appropriate. In Sand Creek, Stan initiated a process of change immediately, during the window of opportunity afforded by the honeymoon period.

In Brewster, Ron found it counterproductive to ask a country church to embrace city ways. In Sand Creek, Stan helped the church to see that an insistence on remaining only a "country church" was contributing to its decline and led it to become a bicultural congregation in which rurbanites could feel at home.

At first glance, these stories may seem to advocate conflicting strategies, but in reality, they embody the same principles in different settings.

1. *Learn your community's culture before promoting major change.* Since Ron was a city slicker moving to the country for the first time, he needed a couple of years to learn ranch culture. Stan, however, had already lived in both rural and urban settings, giving him an insider's feel for both of the cultures.
2. *Shape your ministry to the culture of your community.* Brewster was a ranch town through and through. The better Ron learned to fit into the ranch culture, the more effective his ministry became. Sand Creek had become a bicultural area, including both the farm families who had been there for years as well as the professionals and university students newer to the area. Ministering to the whole community meant becoming a bicultural church.
3. *Pace change to the congregation's readiness for change.* In asking Ron to become their pastor, the only change the Brewster congregation requested was a higher pri-

ority on biblical teaching. Most of the other changes Ron introduced were not in response to any need for change felt by the congregation, so they received only polite responses. All but a few in the Sand Creek congregation felt change was needed to reverse the church's decline, and they looked to Stan to provide leadership in identifying and implementing needed changes.

Both pastors applied the same principles, but their different situations called for different applications of the principles. Before you introduce major changes, study your community's culture. Become a student of the experts in that culture—the people who have lived there longer than you have. With your lay leaders, determine whether your church's way of doing things fits your community today. Then lead your people to explore changes only as you identify actual needs for change.

A Land of Opportunity

Many isolated rural towns are dying and the mood is bleak, but the picture is far different in rurbia. It is exhilarating and challenging to live and work in a modestly growing rurban community where new neighbors keep coming and where new opportunities for ministry keep opening up.

Rurban towns need adventuresome pastors. Since the rurban phenomenon is new, rurban specialists are few. The pastor of the rurban church must be a pioneer, willing to work in unplowed ground with few "policy manuals" to consult. Rurban ministry is bicultural ministry with all the opportunities for conflict and growth that cross-cultural relationships bring.

The migration to rurbia appears to be a trend that will continue well into the twenty-first century, offering a real land of opportunity for ministry for decades to come.

5

Adjust or Bust

Shortly after Roxy and I moved to Brewster, some folks in our church had us over for dinner and served us noodles on mashed potatoes. It sounded awful and looked even worse. Today it is one of my favorite dishes. In fact, the farm wife who first fixed it for us now serves it every time we visit, because she knows how much I like it.

Adapting to the host culture is essential for effective cross-cultural ministry. Missions professor Ray Badgero of Moody Bible Institute captures how critical it is with the slogan, "Adjust or bust!"

Those who are determined to adjust will adopt the new culture as their own. But adopting a new culture involves a lot more than learning to like the local foods and replacing your city clothes with jeans and seed corn jackets—though these things were important for me to do. Missions specialist Paul Hiebert explains:

> In relating to another people we need . . . to deal with our feelings that distinguish between "us" and "our kind of people," and "them" and "their kind of people." Identification takes place only when "they" become part of the circle of people we think of as "our kind of people."[1]

Not everyone who pastors in a small town has to adjust to a new culture, of course. Many pastors of small-town churches grew up in small towns themselves. But even pastors with small-town roots may find cross-cultural relationships critical to their ministries if they are serving in towns different from their home towns. (A small town ten miles from home might have a distinctly different culture). Or, they may be serving in towns that, like Sand Creek in the previous chapter, are becoming bicultural rurban communities.

Adjusting to a new culture takes time, usually one to five years. And Roxy and I found that the process went through several stages.

1. The How-Quaint Phase. This phase is short-lived, lasting just a week or two.

Brewster, which has the distinction of being the smallest county seat in the United States, is in one of the most isolated spots in the country. The people there went to great lengths to persuade us we had not arrived at the edge of the world, but I do recall one fellow finally admitting you could see it from there.

Not only was there no shopping mall in town; there wasn't even a grocery store. We had to drive sixty miles to buy a loaf of bread. Because it was too far to run to the store for milk, our milk came from a local rancher's cow.

We knew we were truly in the boonies shortly after we moved, when Roxy's parents called to ask for our street address since UPS wouldn't deliver a package without one. With Dad and Mom on the phone, I ran outside to look for our house number. I couldn't find it. I looked down the street for a street name, but there was no street sign. I ran inside and told Roxy's folks we'd have to call them back. Roxy checked with our neighbor across the street who told her, "We don't have street addresses here. You'll just have to make one up so UPS will deliver to you. Just don't use one hundred—that's my number."

2. The This-Just-Isn't-Like-Home Phase. This phase involves longing for the familiar and feeling critical of the new culture: "Why do they do it that way? It doesn't make any sense!" There may be tears and even depression as you wonder, "Will I ever be happy here?"

In Brewster, Roxy could not work in her profession because there were no nearby jobs in her field. Both of us had to give up living near extended family, and our children had to grow up without grandparents nearby. The forms of entertainment we had taken for granted in Dallas disappeared overnight. There were no professional or college football games. The Ice Capades never came to town. There was no theater. In fact, because of the prohibitive cost of a high-powered antenna, we couldn't even get TV. And, as I've already described in chapter 3, so much about the church—the building, the worship service—was different from what we were used to. It just didn't feel like home.

This phase normally lasts from a few months to a couple of years, though occasional echoes of this phase may continue for up to five years.

3. The It's-Starting-to-Make-Sense Phase. A few months after I arrived in Brewster, the city-ways-are-better attitude I had brought with me began to soften. I was learning the hard way that it is virtually impossible for an individual to change a culture, and that pastors who try will lose. Instead, the pastor must adapt to the culture.

I had expected, for example, that when people found out I was a seminary graduate, they would stand and salute. While I'm still grateful for what I learned in seminary, I quickly learned that formal education doesn't impress rural people. In fact, for many of them, my schooling erected a cultural barrier.

I learned to keep my diplomas in the closet instead of on the wall. And, while it may not be right for you, one of the best things I did was ask people to call me Ron rather than Reverend or Pastor. That helped to keep me off the pedestal.

Adjusting my preaching was tougher. Instead of using the theological terms and Greek words I had become so familiar with in seminary, I had to learn to speak in plain English. What a challenge! But experience confirmed that I communicated best when I found ways to make the complex simple.

While I had more schooling than the people I was pastoring, I came to see that did not mean I was better educated. I was differently educated and in different subjects, but in some areas critical to my ministry, they knew a lot more than I did. They were the experts on the local culture. I had to admit to myself—and to them—that I knew almost nothing about ranch culture and learned to relate to them as a student.

One day as I was riding down the road in a pickup with a cowboy, I pointed to some cattle and, with an I-know-what-I'm-talking-about tone, said, "Those are sure some nice cows." Well, as it turned out, they weren't cows at all. I thought everything with four legs and a tail was a cow, but these were steers. I quickly learned that there are bulls, heifers, and steers, none of which are cows (with the possible exception of heifers, depending on how you look at it).

I had to learn about the futures market, about hedging, and about cattle varieties and breeds. I learned the difference between pickups and trucks. I learned about fertilizers, different types of seed, and crop diseases. I learned that cheat isn't just something you can do on an exam, but also something that shows up in wheat fields. I learned that dinner in the country is the noon meal, and lunch is a between-meal snack.

I found that when the pastor speaks their language, farmers will be interested in listening and learning when that same pastor preaches the Word of God. But even more than learning the language, people like for their pastors to enter their turf, to take an interest in their lives. Paul was right. If you want to win farmers, you must learn to live like a farmer. If you want to reach a hunter for Christ, you develop an interest in hunting.

The more pastors become the students of their people, the more they can impact their lives for good. If we want to reach people for Christ, we must immerse ourselves in their world instead of trying to force them into ours. This is what I learned during our third phase of adjusting to the culture.

As our struggles with the new culture eased, we had fewer critical things to say about the people around us, and we didn't say "This is how we did it back home" as often.

4. *The I-Like-It Phase.* Finally, it's home. You feel settled in your new surroundings. The worst is over. Now you can laugh about those embarrassing moments of cultural adjustment. Going back to your former culture for a visit now seems like just that—a visit. It's not home anymore. In fact, you may come to prefer your adopted culture to the one you left behind.

Moving to another culture has its price, but our family has gained far more than we have given up. What did we gain? For one thing, air that is free of smog and bright city lights. I was shocked to find that the stars can be plainly visible at night.

We gained space. I now feel almost claustrophobic when I visit the city.

We gained a relaxed lifestyle. Small-town people take time to drink coffee together in the local cafe and to visit on the streets, often holding up traffic as they do.

We gained community closeness. In a small town you can dial a wrong number and end up talking for fifteen minutes. You can walk into the variety store, the cafe, or the grocery store, and you're not a nameless face. When our family goes for walks at night, it can take us a couple of hours to go around the block because we stop and visit with so many people.

In the small town, the almost lost art of visiting people in their homes is still going strong. We have spent countless evenings with friends, visiting, watching a football game to-gether, or playing table games, sometimes till the wee hours of the morning.

When we were pastoring in Oklahoma and our children were preschoolers, our family ate brunch at our local cafe every Monday morning. Dirk, the owner of our little cafe, often had a warm apricot pie waiting for me—my favorite. After we gave the waitress our order, which always included pancakes for our kids, Dirk would usually walk out from behind the grill calling, "I need a pancake flipper." Our children, Caleb and

Charissa, would jump off their chairs and follow Dirk behind the grill like two ducklings behind their mama. For years, Caleb's ambition was to be a cafe cook just like Dirk.

Besides community closeness, we have also gained community spirit. Roxy and I thought going to a Cowboys game was fun when we lived in Dallas. But now that we've lived in several small towns, we'd take our high school football games over the Dallas Cowboys anytime. Community spirit is contagious in the small town.

Best of all, we have gained family togetherness, something we found hard to maintain amid splintered family interests in the city. We have learned we don't have to go to the Ice Capades or the circus to have a good time together. Sunday afternoon rodeoing on someone else's ranch can be every bit as much fun. Our family plays together; we go to the park; we have picnics; we often invite people into our home. We've learned to be creative with family activities; the alternative is to sit on the porch and watch the grass grow.

Our family has grown to love small-town life and today, even apart from ministry considerations, we prefer to live in a small town. It's home now.

We can do things to help, hinder, or even completely stop our progress through these stages of cultural adjustment. Because they fail to adjust, some pastors move on before making a significant contribution to the life of the church. Perhaps even more unfortunate, they leave before they have had a chance to learn what the church can teach them.

What can you do to ease your transition to a new culture?

Get out with the people. A new culture can be threatening. It is tempting to hide in the pastor's study. After all, good sermons are the key to your church's growth—right? Wrong! Good preaching is important, but most people come into the church through relationships. Discipline yourself to get out of the office. Find the centers of socialization in your community—perhaps the local cafe or the school football game—then spend time there.

Become a student of the culture. What is important to the people? What rituals are important to the community? Is there a discernible power structure?

Withhold judgment. Just because a way of life is different from what you are used to doesn't mean it is wrong. Keep an open mind. In time you may come to appreciate what seemed odd to you at first.

Remember the reason. While there is much to gain by becoming bicultural, you also lose some things in the process. These sacrifices come more easily when we remember the reason for them: "I have become all things to all men so that by all possible means I might save some" (1 Cor. 9:22). This motive, the same motive that compelled Jesus to bridge the greatest cultural gap ever as he left home to become flesh and take up residence with sinful humanity, will enable us to say to those with whom we live: "Your town is my town."

Part III

Building on Small-Church Strengths

❦ 6 ❦

Use Your Two *I*'s

Have you ever wondered why so many small rural churches are pictured on Christmas cards? How often do you see Christmas cards that feature the facilities of megachurches? Why do you suppose these images of small churches evoke feelings that pictures of large church buildings cannot?

When people say, "We don't want to go to this church—it's too big," what are they saying? And why do you suppose seminars and books for the megachurch often focus on how to make the large church feel small?

Conventional wisdom has it that big churches are better than small churches because they can do so much more. After all, what small church can put together a mass choir? How many small churches can afford to hire a youth pastor, a children's director, a director of senior adult ministries, or a full-time minister of music?

But there is a reason rural church buildings end up on Christmas cards, and megachurch facilities do not. What is it that seems to come naturally to the small church but is hard for large churches to duplicate?

Obviously, large churches can do some things best. But just as clearly, there are some things small churches can do best.

For the small church to fulfill its potential, it must know what it does best and capitalize on its strengths.

Big Tractor, Little Tractor

Most farmers have at least two tractors, one large, the other small. The large tractor is better for some jobs, the small tractor for others. Trying to mow a ditch along the road with a big tractor is an exercise in frustration, but a small tractor can do the job handily. Using a small tractor to plow a large field wastes many hours, but a large tractor makes short work of it. The smart farmer uses each tractor for the jobs it can do best.

Many small churches make the mistake of trying to copy the large church, simply scaling its programs down. Most large churches, for example, have choirs, so the small church may decide to have a choir, even if it only has five people in it and four can't carry a tune. (One small-church pastor fondly described his church's five-member choir as "one flat, one sharp, and three undecided.") But even if all five choir members can sing, they cannot do the job of a large-church choir. Suppose two ads appear in your paper at Christmastime. One reads, "Come hear our five-voice choir sing." The other says, "Come hear our one-hundred-voice choir and full orchestra." Which would you want to hear?

Just as it would be foolish to use a small tractor to do a big tractor's job, it is counterproductive to try to imitate large-church programs in small churches. The small church that tries to be a scaled-down version of a big church will become a pale imitation of a large church. The church will feel—and be—inferior to the larger churches it is copying. Why would anyone want to attend a second-rate imitation of a large church?

Just as the small tractor is most effective when it does the work it's designed for, the small church has the greatest impact when it doesn't try to act like a big church but focuses on doing those things small churches do best. And what are those things? They can be summarized in two words—intimacy and involvement.

The First *I*—Intimacy

While the large church scrambles to find ways to encourage warmth and personal relationships, the small church, if it is healthy, quite naturally has a family atmosphere. Large churches have to create small-group ministries; in the small church, many small-group dynamics occur naturally. Big churches ask guests to fill out a card so an assigned person can visit them that week; in most small churches, people spontaneously greet those who visit their services. In the large church, many faces are unfamiliar; in the small church, everyone knows everyone else.

The pastor of a small church looks out the window and says, "Jim, you left your lights on." In a large church, an usher passes a note to the pastor who then announces, "A brown Ford, license number TM3527, has its lights on."

Anyone who has belonged to a healthy small church will recall many stories illustrating the warmth and intimacy that normally characterize the small-town church. In one Minnesota church, for example, the elementary-age girl who was providing the special music forgot the words to the song she was singing. At first the congregation chuckled sympathetically. As she struggled to remember and start again, the people began to hum softly, adding their voices to hers. Reassured by the sound of friends and family, she finished the hymn and was rewarded by the beaming smiles and sincere applause of the congregation.

One of our favorite memories of small-town hospitality is of the holiday we (Ron and Roxy) awoke to find ourselves snowed in and with no electricity or phone due to the storm. Church friends had invited us to spend the day at their home, but with the roads buried under knee-deep snow, we resigned ourselves to spending a lonely day at home.

We were feeling disappointed and depressed when, about noon, we were surprised to hear a knock at our back door. There stood the twenty-one-year-old son of our friends. He and his dad had spent the last four hours on two tractors, clearing the way from their ranch to the main road so they could get to our house.

This warm friendliness is a big part of what large churches are trying to recreate when they try to cultivate a small-church atmosphere.

The Second *I*—Involvement

While many in the large church are spectators, in the small church, active participation is a given. As the number of people in an organization goes up, the natural tendency is for the level of participation to go down. It is not unusual for 80 percent or more of the members of a small church to have specific ministry responsibilities in the church. Most larger churches feel fortunate if 30 to 40 percent of their members accept specific ministry assignments.

Before Scott and Lyn moved into our area and began worshiping at Valley Chapel, they attended a larger congregation of about three hundred. Though they had grown up in their previous church, neither of them had been very involved in its ministries. When I asked why, they told me they never felt like they were really needed there.

They both quickly became deeply involved in Valley Chapel's ministry. Lyn began working with several of our children's ministries and later volunteered to type the church bulletin. Scott became a leader in our midweek children's program and used his mechanical skills to keep the church's lawn mower in shape.

Unlike Scott and Lyn, Ed was not a church attender when he came in contact with Valley Chapel. He had grown up with several of the church's members and had carefully observed the gospel's impact in their lives. After their children began attending Valley Chapel's vacation Bible school and Sunday school, Ed's wife, Cindy, trusted in Christ, but Ed kept his distance. In time, though, he was won over by the testimony of his friends.

After his conversion, Ed followed their example and became involved in the life of the church, at first working mostly with building maintenance. He often shared the gospel with his friends and coworkers and invited them to church events. As Ed's faith grew, his involvement expanded as well. He is now a member of the board of elders and teaches Sunday school. When asked why he got involved so early in his Christian experience, he answered, "I thought that's what everybody did."

One key to the small church's effectiveness is in resisting the temptation to become a scaled-down imitation of the large church and instead capitalizing on the small church's greatest strengths—intimacy and involvement. To some extent, this may happen spontaneously, but you can also intentionally build on these qualities, beginning with your preaching and style of worship.

Interactive Preaching

Think about the last sermon you heard in a large church. Did the preacher stand at the same level as the audience or above them, looking down? What size was the pulpit? Was the delivery one-way or did the preacher and worshipers dialogue? What "voice" did the preacher use—formal, conversational, "preachy"?

Though it varies from church to church, we usually associate an elevated platform, a massive pulpit, one-way delivery, and a formal or a preachy delivery with large-church sermons. The very physical arrangement of a large sanctuary emphasizes formality. It suggests separation of pastor from congregation. When pastors of small churches imitate this big-church style of preaching, they are creating distance between themselves and the people and undermining the small-church quality of intimacy.

But you can develop an approach to preaching that builds on and nurtures the intimacy of the small church. Instead of preaching from behind a pulpit, for example, why not use a small lectern—or no lectern at all?

In the small church, why promote separation by elevating the pastor? Why can't the pastor speak on the same level as the congregation or elevated only slightly if necessary for visibility?

Why should the preacher use a preachy tone of voice, a practice that sets the preacher apart from the people? Why not use the same conversational voice used between friends? Wouldn't that do more to create an atmosphere of friendliness? Why be limited to a one-way delivery? Why not open up the communication to include the kind of dialogue typical of a healthy family?

In all these ways, preaching in the small church can be tailored to enhance the small-church strengths of intimacy and involvement.[1]

What style of preaching did you learn in Bible college or seminary? Most of us learned a large-church preaching style. Yet if you look at the sermons of Jesus, Peter, or Paul in the New Testament, you'll find lots of dialogue, object lessons, and storytelling. It may require us to retrain ourselves, but it is possible to learn a preaching style that promotes intimacy and involvement.

Use object lessons. Matthew 5:39 says, "If someone strikes you on the right cheek, turn to him the other also." Ask, "Have you ever wondered why Jesus says 'right cheek'? Why not 'left cheek'? Or why not just 'cheek'?"

Then ask a child to come up. (Do you remember when Jesus did this?) Ask the child which is his or her right cheek, then show how a right-handed person would have to slap a person to slap the right cheek—backhanded. A backhand slap in that culture was an insult. So what Christ is teaching here is how to respond to an insult.

That's interactive preaching. The informality (intimacy) and involvement combine to make this kind of preaching more powerful.

Ask a question and invite responses. In 1 Samuel 16:1–2 God encourages Samuel to tell a lie. Is lying sometimes acceptable? Colossians 3:20 says children should obey their parents in everything. Ask, "Does 'everything' really mean everything? Are there exceptions?" Leviticus 19:18 says, "Love your neighbor as yourself." Ask your congregation, "What are some specific ways we can do this?"

Allow time for the congregation to ask questions. When I (Ron) started doing this following my Sunday morning sermons, the response was far better than I anticipated. This puts intimacy and involvement center stage and guarantees spontaneous variety.

Occasionally I've been asked questions I couldn't answer on the spot. Sometimes when that happens a member of the congregation is able to field the question. Other times I've promised to work on the question during the week and be prepared to talk about it the following Sunday.

Ask a member to prepare a testimony that shows how the biblical principle you are preaching on has worked in real life. When a lady shared one Sunday about how God sustained her family during her husband's cancer treatments, her testimony was far more powerful than any abstract teaching the pastor could do about how God takes care of us in trying times.

Call in the experts in advance to help you prepare your sermon. Invite members of your congregation to meet with you a couple of weeks before your sermon. Tell them your text and the principle you will be preaching on and ask how it relates to them. Probe for specific applications. Once when the topic was "love your enemy," a church member related this story to his pastor:

A sheep farmer lived next to a wheat farmer who had some large dogs. The dogs were scaring the sheep, and the sheep farmer didn't know what to do. Should he shoot the dogs? Poison them? Take his neighbor to court?

When he prayed about it a solution occurred to him. As soon as the new lambs were born, he gave each of his neighbor's children a lamb for a pet. They were thrilled. And their father couldn't allow the dogs to keep running wild but had to restrain them for the sake of the pet lambs. The two enemies became friends.

Since the pastor had never been a farmer, it is unlikely he would ever have come up with a story like that on his own.

Calling in the experts enables you to move beyond abstract problems with generic solutions and incorporate into your sermons real-life problems with real solutions. And if you mention who gave you the illustration (with permission, of course), you further demonstrate that your people are partners in your preaching ministry.

Invite spontaneous sharing in response to the sermon. One Sunday, after a sermon on assurance of salvation, a lady who had struggled with this area for years said, "This issue is important. I know I didn't start growing as a Christian until I settled it. I kept looking back at my salvation instead of looking forward to my need for spiritual growth."

Later that week another member of the congregation sent a card to the pastor, thanking him for the helpful message, but clearly her greatest help came not from the sermon itself, but from the sharing by her friend.

After one Sunday's sermon, a middle-aged divorced man said through his tears, "If I had known twenty years ago some of the things I heard this morning, my first marriage wouldn't have failed. I hope the teenagers here are listening and that the younger couples will apply these principles so their marriages won't end like mine did."

A hush fell over the congregation, and eyes everywhere were moist. That sermon was cemented in the hearts of the young people.

These people who spoke were not merely responding to the sermon; by adding their life experiences to the preaching of the Word, they were actively participating in the preaching.

Creatively involve others in delivering the sermon. Use puppets or drama. Send someone to the school library to research a topic and make a report to the congregation.

One pastor preached a sermon that frequently repeated one word. Before beginning the sermon, he offered a prize to the child who counted the most uses of that word in his sermon. In one congregation, a member with excellent photography skills used her photography to introduce and enhance sermons or even give an entire "sermon with slides."

Moving from a "big church" preaching style to an interactive approach will increase the impact of your preaching ministry. But just as it took time for you to develop your present preaching style, it will take time to develop a new one. Don't give up if your first few attempts don't go as smoothly as you'd like. Keep practicing until you become as comfortable with your new way of preaching as you were with your old one.

Participatory Worship

We have often heard pastors of small churches complain about what their churches cannot do in their worship services because of their size. They groan that they cannot match the quality of worship of a large church. But with worship, as with every other area, the small church makes a huge mistake if it tries to copy the large church. Rather, the small church needs to shape its worship to capitalize on intimacy and involvement.

In no other area is the small church tempted to feel inferior to the large church more frequently than in the area of music. We look at megachurches and see their large choirs, keyboard artists, and great talent, and we think, "If only we had just a little bit of that in our church."

Gary Roseboom, who has served as the minister of music in several large churches, offers an interesting perspective on the different roles of music in large and small churches. Through his large-church experiences, he has become weary of the performance mentality of many in the big church. In fact, he often finds the small-church atmosphere to be more conducive to authentic worship.

In the big church, what you often have is entertainment, and the audience thinks of worship as something you sit back and enjoy. Under these conditions, it is difficult to truly worship. What bothers Gary is the number of churches that are trying to imitate the large-church performance approach to worship instead of appreciating and making the most of the intimacy and involvement that enhance authentic worship in the small church.

Good worship is not a fancy sound system or a choir or talented soloists or professional instrumentalists. The best worship is simply when all the people participate in ascribing worth to God.

What are some of the practical implications of this understanding of worship?

Choirs or ensembles. We've already noted that since big churches have big choirs, small churches may feel they should have small choirs. But if that doesn't work, what does? Since a choir is not essential for worship, one good option is simply to not have a choir. Another possibility is to have a smaller singing group but not call it a choir; call it an ensemble, or give the group a name. One small church calls its singing group the Amazing Grace Singers.

A lack of musical training need not be a barrier. There is a lot of choir and ensemble music available through your music store that is specifically designed to be simple to sing.

Special vocal music. The big church lets people on the platform only if they can sing well. If the small church follows that policy, most of the time there won't be special music. This flies in the face of involvement.

Dr. Warren Wiersbe describes the attitude called for in the small church:

> If the players and singers are doing their best, and seeking to do better, then God accepts their "sacrifices of praise" and so should we. . . . Whenever I am listening to a below-average presentation, I imagine my Lord receiving it and presenting it to the Father; and that changes my attitude completely. . . . Learn to appreciate the best, but do not become a religious highbrow who is above listening to anything but the best.[2]

Special music by children. The small church should invite children to play instruments or sing, even though their music is less than perfect. Everyone forgives children when they make mistakes. Plus, parents will think, "If our family was in a large church, they would not let my daughter play a piano solo."

Special music by families. The small church should encourage families to do special music together. Both of us have
heard family music presentations that, though full of imper-
fections, connected powerfully with the audience. To the small
church's credit, the congregation is more interested in giving
people opportunities to participate than it is in judging those
who participate.

But does this create a problem for those with considerable
musical talent? To these, Dr. Wiersbe says:

> I can understand that a gifted musician might want a greater
> challenge and opportunity. I can also understand how frustrat-
> ing it must be to practice weekly with less-talented people. How-
> ever, keep in mind that you have a contribution to make right
> where you are. If you have a servant's heart, you will use your
> exceptional gifts to build others and not yourself.[3]

Congregational singing. The small church should have fre-
quent informal times of singing. Perhaps the small church cannot have a mass choir, but neither can the large church sing
around the piano. The small church should try to avoid the rut
of always announcing a hymn then asking everyone to stand
to sing it. This may work well in the large church (though even
large churches are moving away from it), but it works against
the informal atmosphere of the small church.

Consider singing with more spontaneity, perhaps in blocks
of time, instead of one song at a time. For best participation,
choose the most "singable" songs. For some people, these will
be hymns; for others, more contemporary choruses. Sing what
your congregation sings best. If you have variety in your congregation, sing a variety of kinds of music. Slides or overhead
projectors can make songs more singable, because people are
looking up to sing instead of burying their heads in hymn books.

Many small churches have excellent congregational singing,
far better than what you find in many larger churches. This
happens when the singing is conducted in ways that promote
intimacy and involvement.

Instrumental music. The small church must also avoid trying to imitate the large church's use of musical instruments. In many large churches, for example, the piano is isolated and the accompanist's back is to the audience. This may be appropriate in a large church, but to do the same thing in a small church works against the feeling of warmth and intimacy you want in your worship.

Because the big church has a big organ, many small churches think they need a small organ. But many smaller organs produce a funeral-dirge sound hardly conducive to worship. Besides, an organ tends to encourage formality instead of the informality that ought to be the strength of the small church.

The small church can't afford and doesn't need a large organ. But most can afford an electronic keyboard. An electronic keyboard costs less than most small organs, and it offers a great sound with incredible versatility. It can sound like a full church organ, a piano, or a host of other instruments. Because it is not imposing and formal, it contributes to an atmosphere of intimacy. And because it is less intimidating than an organ, more people in your congregation are likely to be willing to play it, increasing involvement.

If you don't have a good keyboard person who can play a prelude, you might have preservice congregational singing of choruses. Or you could play a compact disk of prelude music.

Leading worship. Consider having a worship team of several people who share in leading worship. The small church can and should encourage broad participation in all parts of the worship service, such as Scripture reading, praying, and taking the offering. Young people especially should be encouraged to take part. Not only does this say to the youth that the service is for them as well as the adults, but it also is excellent training for future ministry. Constantly remind your people that "our church is a place that trains young people."

A disproportionate percentage of professional Christian workers, including as many as 80 percent of foreign missionaries, come from small churches. Why? Because small churches have a much higher rate of involvement, and this prepares young people for future service. Ask small-churchers what they have contributed to missions and they'll tell you with a mixture of pride and sadness: our kids.

Sharing times. Small churches can easily include testimonies and sharing times in their services. In our impersonal world, people feel a deep need to have a place to share their experiences, yet such sharing is almost impossible in the large-church worship service. In the small church, personal sharing in the services can sometimes lead to powerful ministry.

One Sunday, Dave and Sarah came to the evening service looking worn and discouraged. Everyone in their small church knew why. The week before, Dave's mother had suffered a stroke and had been committed to a nursing home. Sarah had to make a quick trip out of state to attend the funeral of her aunt. Sensing their need, during the service the pastor asked everyone to come to the front and form a circle around Dave and Sarah, to join hands, and to pray that God would strengthen and encourage them.

Order of service. Dare we touch on a sacred cow? The church bulletin includes a formal listing of the order of service. This works well in a church that emphasizes formality but it hinders the church that is trying to cultivate more spontaneity and informality. Could the quality of your worship be enhanced by dispensing with an order of service?

Advance planning. Encouraging spontaneity doesn't mean no planning should go into the services. We've all been in services where the music and the sermon are totally unrelated; the music might be in a minor key while the sermon is on positive thinking. One way to maximize the limited resources of a small congregation is to plan worship services well in advance. We suggest developing a calendar of services several months ahead. With advance planning, the music, prayers, readings, and drama can all relate to a single theme. We cannot expect wholehearted and broadly based involvement in leading worship if participants are given only a few days' notice to prepare.

While the large church may tend to define competency in terms of professional-quality skills, in the small church, competency consists of making the most of intimacy and involvement. Don't try to remake your church in the image of the large church. In a world where most people feel like faces in the crowd, many are longing for intimacy more than polished performance, for involvement more than spectator status, for small rather than big. By specializing in doing well what the small church does best, your church can be there for people who are hungering for a personal touch in an impersonal age.

7

The Great Niche Hunt

In a day when megachurches offer a full array of services, how is the small church to survive? Why would anyone attend a small church when just twenty minutes away is a big church with a full-blown music program, a counseling center, various kinds of recovery groups, and a full schedule of activities for every age group from preschool through senior adults?

This situation isn't imaginary. It's real. And it's tempting for people in small churches to respond to it with an if-only attitude: If only we had more people. If only we had more money. If only we had more musical talent. If only we had more singles. "We're just a little church," the thinking goes. "We can't do much."

It's true, of course, that the small church can't do everything the large church does. But that doesn't mean the small church has to settle for second-rate ministries. At Valley Chapel, it was by accident that we stumbled across the secret of operating top-quality ministries in the small church.

Stumbling into Success

On my son's first day of kindergarten, I (John) stood at the curb with Drew waiting for the bus. I think I was more anxious than he was. Would he like school? Was his teacher nice? How would the older children on the bus treat him?

When the bus finally rolled to a stop with its lights flashing, I blinked back tears and waved good-bye as Drew climbed aboard. To my amazement, a chorus of voices rose as one child after another called to me.

"Hi, Pastor John."

"Hey, Pastor John."

"Pastor, remember me?"

As I scanned the faces, I was surprised to recognize many of them from our Sunday school, vacation Bible school, or our midweek children's program.

Through the years Valley Chapel has become known for its strong children's programs. We have developed a "niche" ministry.

Specialization has long been recognized as an effective strategy in the business world. It has been the key to success for many small businesses that fill a niche left by other larger companies. The small church that develops niche ministries that are sensitive to the needs of the unchurched can reach out to people whose specific needs are not being addressed by other nearby churches, either large or small.

The truth is that no church of any size can meet all the needs around it. But any church can do those things God has specifically called it to do. God never calls us to do anything without also giving us the resources to do it, though the call will often come before the resources do.

Researcher George Barna has observed that the most effective churches deliberately limit their ministries, focusing on those specific areas for which they have resources and in which they have the ability to serve with excellence.[1] If even large churches have to observe this principle to be effective, how much more do small churches whose resources are even more limited need to follow it?

How did Valley Chapel find its niche? Was it through careful market research or my insightful leadership? I would like to say yes. In reality, however, it was an accident. Valley Chapel never really set out to be a "kid friendly" church. Initially, our vacation Bible school and Sunday school programs were primarily focused on the children in our own congregation. Our midweek children's ministry was begun by a couple who wanted to see their children involved in such a ministry. But as more people got involved, the vision for these programs grew. Later, when I reflected on our success, I realized we had unwittingly combined two key elements.

First, our children's programs allowed the members of our church to minister in an area of great interest to them. One of the things that puzzled me at first about our church's ministry niche was that it did not reflect my own interests. But many of our church's members are educators, and this ministry reflects their interest in children.

Second, we had tapped into a perceived need in the community. When members of our congregation recently surveyed friends and neighbors, those surveyed overwhelmingly identified family as their number one concern. Parents in particular were worried about the values their children were adopting. Even many who did not see church as an important feature in their own lives wanted to see their children involved in church.

The principle of niche ministry Valley Chapel stumbled on by accident is one that any church can follow by design. But it does call for a new way of thinking about programming.

Step 1: Start with Gifts

There are at least two fundamentally different ways to approach programming in the church, and these tend to grow out of two different motivations. As pastor, I need to ask myself why I want people to be involved in the ministries of the church.

The first possible motivation is *employment:* I want them to help me achieve my ministry goals. In this model, the lay leaders serve the pastor. Understandably, members who feel I am using them as tools to accomplish my goals are often reluctant to cooperate. Jesus' observation about the Sabbath applies equally to the programs of the church: Programs were made for people, not people for programs (cf. Mark 2:27).

The second possible motivation is *empowerment*. In this model, the pastor serves the members of the church. The pastor is motivated by a desire to see them find fulfillment in Christ by helping them discern God's call and develop their full ministry potential. When people know I am more interested in helping them fulfill their potential than in getting them to help me reach my goals, they feel valued, not used.

How does this affect the way we staff ministries? Perhaps the most common approach to staffing the church's ministries is to begin with programs, then recruit people to fill positions to run the programs. With this approach, unless great care is taken, the workers can end up serving the programs.

A more effective—and more biblical—approach is to start not with programs, but with spiritual gifts. Instead of setting programs in place first and then staffing them with the reluctant, the disinterested, or the ill-suited, we can begin by designing programs around people's spiritual gifts, interests, and abilities. This will mean that when God does not call people to fill vacancies in a particular program, rather than pressuring people to fill slots, we make changes in the program, so it doesn't become a burdensome duty for those God is actually calling to do something else. People should never serve programs; programs should be tools that enable people to better fulfill their calls.

One church in Red Hill, Pennsylvania, realized it didn't have enough children's workers to offer both Sunday school and children's church, so it streamlined its children's ministry. It designed a Sunday morning service that lasted ninety minutes. The first half of the service is for both adults and children, consisting of lively singing, sharing, prayer, and announcements. Then the children are dismissed to have Sunday school while the adults listen to the sermon.

Creative programming such as this can keep a particular ministry program in scale with the number of workers God has provided to do it. Those not called to that ministry are not pressed into service, but are left free to follow God's call in other areas, perhaps areas of ministry in which the church is not yet involved.

When members enter ministry motivated by an awareness of their own gifts and call, rather than from a sense of obligation to keep a program running, the programs of the church will come to be shaped around the members' gifts. New programs will spring up, some existing programs will grow, others will be reshaped, and yet others will become smaller or, when they have served their purposes, come to an end.

This approach to programming can lead to the identification of "gift clusters" in the congregation. A gift cluster is a grouping of spiritual gifts usually found in the church's strongest ministries. Though Valley Chapel has specialized in ministry to children, the gifts and interests in some churches may cluster around music and worship, while other churches will shine in teen ministries or community service. By identifying the gift clusters in the congregation, the small church can approach its ministry confident that God has equipped it to serve its community in a unique way.

Step 2: Identify Needs

Effective ministry in the small congregation begins with an understanding of where its spiritual gifts and ministry passion lie. What is the church best equipped to do? This understanding must be complemented by an understanding of your church's ministry environment. What does your mission field look like? Demographic information, much of it available at your public library, can often provide an eye-opening profile of your community.

Lyle Schaller recommends that the church considering a specialized ministry ask itself three questions:

- Who are the people in this general community who are overlooked by the churches?
- What are their needs?
- To which of these needs could we respond if we decided to make the effort?[2]

A church can come up with a long list of things it would like to do. There are fewer things the members of the congregation actually have the gifts to do. The list narrows even further when you ask what needs around you God is calling you to respond to.

When you find the place where the gifts and ministry passion of a group of members intersect with the needs of the community, that is where you find an answer to the question: What is God calling our church to do?

It would be convenient if such a call were always as clear as Paul's Macedonian vision (Acts 16:9–10). Most, however, discover it gradually, as the church experiments with first one ministry, then another, until it discovers those that resonate with both congregation and community.

Freedom to Experiment

Since discerning call involves experimentation, the pastor and other leaders must create an environment within the church where people feel free to take risks. A person proposing a new ministry should not feel obligated to prove in advance that the ministry is likely to succeed. People who are trying to identify their gifts can be invited to serve in a ministry on a trial basis as a part of the process of discerning whether God is calling them to work in the ministry long-term. Those taking on a ministry for the first time must know they are not expected to demonstrate the same level of competence as those who have ten or twenty years' experience.

Pastors who want their congregation to be on the cutting edge of creative ministry must help nurture an atmosphere that encourages experimentation. Thomas Edison performed fifty thousand experiments before he discovered the right elements that enabled him to develop a new storage battery. When asked if he was frustrated that so little had resulted from so much work, the inventor replied, "Results? Why, I have gotten a lot of results. I know fifty thousand things that won't work."

Whether an experiment demonstrates that something does work or doesn't work, that a certain ministry is or is not a good match for the person or the church, the experiment is a success because it tells the experimenter what he or she was trying to find out.

Perfectionism—demanding excellence—can kill creativity. Paradoxically it is by extending the freedom to fail—by creating an atmosphere where the inexperienced can develop new skills without feeling embarrassed by their mistakes and where those with vision are encouraged to experiment with new ministries—that you provide the environment that is most likely to lead to excellence in ministry.

A Case Study

One of the best contemporary examples of finding a niche and filling it is the story of Wal-Mart. We believe the small-town church can learn from its example.

Many people look at small towns and isolated areas and see no potential. Sam Walton saw potential. In his autobiography, Walton writes: "Our key strategy . . . was simply to put . . . discount stores into little one-horse towns which everybody else was ignoring. . . . When people want to simplify the Wal-Mart story, that's usually how they sum up the secret of our success:

'Oh, they went into small towns when nobody else would.'"[3] Sam Walton saw potential that almost everyone else passed over.

Many small churches in small towns are struggling because they see no potential. Two pastors can look at the same town, and where one sees no hope for a strong church, the other visualizes a thriving church. Guess which pastor will end up with the healthy church?

In his book Walton describes the decline of many small towns of years gone by. Small-town stores closed, and Main Streets were deserted. The remaining residents didn't hesitate to drive a few miles to a discount store in a larger town to save a few bucks. Most people saw no potential for changing this pattern, but Sam Walton did.

Pastors can do the same. Pastors can enter declining towns and strategically develop a church that has so much to offer that the people of that community wouldn't think of going a few miles to the next town to attend church.

The coming of Wal-Mart to many small towns presented, for some, a challenge of a different stripe: How could the small business on Main Street compete with a large discount store? This challenge is not unlike that of the small church that struggles because a large church in the next town can offer a fuller range of ministries. In a candid portion of his book, Walton suggests how those small businesses can survive—and even thrive—though a Wal-Mart is just down the road.[4]

"They need to avoid coming at us head-on." There's no way the small store can win that one. Neither can the small church. The small church must find ways to be distinctly different (see chapter 6) instead of trying to imitate the large church.

"They need to . . . do their own thing better than we do ours." That is, they need to find a need the mass merchandiser is unable to meet and supply it. For instance a small-store owner can get out on the floor and meet customers, let them know how much he appreciates them, and ring that cash register himself. People will come back because they want to shop in a store where they can be in touch with the owner.

Sam Walton can't do this with every Wal-Mart customer. Neither can a megachurch pastor. But, the small-church pastor can have close relationships with his congregation and his community. A hardware store in a small town can compete with Wal-Mart because it staffs people who take time to listen to customers' plumbing problems and provide tips for fixing them. Wal-Mart can't do this. Neither can the megachurch. But the small church can.

Offer a specialized line of products Wal-Mart can't offer. Walton points out that many Ben Franklin stores converted to craft specialty shops when they realized they could not stay in business as variety stores with Wal-Mart in the same town. Says Walton, "I don't care how many Wal-Marts come to town, there are always niches that we can't reach."

We see small churches doing just this. One church we know of caters to a Western lifestyle: they sponsor roping events, rodeo Bible camps, and cook-outs. Another church has several people skilled in drama. Every year they put on a Passion play during Easter week, which thousands attend. Churches that find a niche become known for it.

"Business conditions change, and . . . survivors have to adapt to those changing conditions." Walton refuses to take "credit" for shutting down smaller stores in town. He says these stores brought it on themselves by refusing to change. The application to the small church is obvious.

Think small. Knowing that his customers had small-town values, Walton did his best to make his stores personal, folksy, and family-like.

Involve the people. All who work at Wal-Mart see their roles as vital because of many incentives and ownership options. Walton went to great lengths to make every Wal-Mart associate (their term for employee) feel an integral part of the business. Doing the same in your congregation will enhance the small-church strength of involvement.

Be enthusiastic. Walton was famous for his rallies, stock market shareholders' meetings, and Saturday staff meetings. He was constantly pointing out the company's victories. Likewise, small-church pastors best motivate their congregations by celebrating what is, rather than moaning about what should be.

Monitor what you are doing. Walton developed an incredibly precise system of monitoring what was happening in every Wal-Mart store. He kept tabs on how every venture was doing. This meant all his employees knew where they were going and how far along they were toward getting there. Emerging problems were nipped in the bud. Churches need to do the same, rather than practicing crisis management.[5]

Walton made a success of planting stores in small towns by finding a niche other businesses had overlooked. High-growth people didn't understand him—just like many church-growth experts today may not see all the possibilities for small-town growth.

It's all a matter of being able to see potential—and finding the right niche.

8

Secrets of Small-Church Leadership

I (Ron) was taught a lot about church leadership in seminary. I was taught how to preach and how to guard my study hours, so I could preach my best. I was taught how to conduct services. I was taught how to lead meetings. I was taught how to administer. In short I was taught how to be a CEO.

So when I started my first pastorate, I felt well-prepared to do all these things. I spent long hours in my study every week preparing sermons and as a result probably preached some of the best sermons the congregation had ever heard. I used the skills I had developed to make our worship services run more smoothly than ever before. I worked at administration, ensuring that every church event was organized to a *T.* I loved it all, and I did it well.

Yet my ministry was going nowhere. People were sitting through my sermons and taking part in the events I organized, but I could see that these sermons and events weren't making much difference in people's lives. I was doing what I had been taught. Why wasn't it working?

Leadership Models: Business versus Family

As you know from chapter 3, what I learned was that my effectiveness as the pastor of the Brewster church had little to do with how well I preached or led worship or administered, though those things all had their place. My effectiveness as pastor was determined primarily by my personal relationships with the people.

Effectiveness came only when I started spending less time in my study and more time in the local cafe drinking coffee. It came when I spent less time organizing church events and more time touring members' businesses or having lunch with them. It came when I got out of the office and went to ball games or went hunting. I learned that an hour of personal time with someone in my congregation could have more impact than a dozen sermons.

Because I am a behind-the-desk person, I had to block off on my calendar several hours a week for relationships, so I wouldn't just drift toward desk work, which came easier for me. And because I am shy, I had to work at developing people skills. But the more I worked at it, the easier it got and the more I enjoyed it. Once I started regularly investing time in building relationships, it wasn't long before church members started viewing me as a member of the family instead of as an outsider.

The CEO model of church leadership I had learned in seminary, I came to realize, really didn't fit the small-town church. While a large church may operate much like a business and so need a pastor with strong business skills, the small church sees itself more as a family. The pastor's role, therefore, is less that of a CEO, and more that of a nurturing parent. More than anything else, what the small church wants in a pastor is someone who will love them.

The following chart highlights some of the differences between CEO and parent styles of leadership.

CEO (business model)	Parent (family model)
More authoritarian	More on their level
More directive	More input from everyone
More distant	More personal, relational
More organizational, formal	More spontaneous, informal

While the megachurch cannot govern itself as a family, the small church tends to make decisions more like families do—with the whole church involved. While some pastors of successful small churches work more like CEOs, small churches are usually best served by a family model of leadership in which relational skills are valued more highly than business skills.

Management by Relationship

Churches need strong pastoral leadership to cast vision and provide the kind of direction that will help them steer clear of the innate tendencies that can stifle their growth and development. They need leaders who can function effectively as change agents. But when many small-church pastors propose needed changes, they see their ideas rejected. Some pastors respond by accusing their members of being set in their ways, unenlightened, uneducated, or uncommitted. But blaming doesn't get the job done.

When change is needed, how do you go about building support for it?

Step 1: Build relationships. The authority to lead does not come with the position of pastor; you have to earn it through winning your people's trust. The first step in earning that trust is to build strong, warm, family-like relationships. If you don't yet have such relationships, you may as well put your idea on hold and work on relationships first.

Relationship is the precondition for change. Effective small-church leadership depends on pastor and people learning to deeply trust one another and work closely as partners. If your people like you, if they trust you, they will like your ideas. In leadership just as in every other area of small-church life, intimacy and involvement are the keys.

Step 2: Find the right way to initiate change. The degree of initiative churches want their pastors to take tends to vary with the size of the church. Lyle Schaller divides small churches into three basic organizational types:

   a. The fellowship of less than 35 or 40 uses an informal decision-making process much like that of the small group. The individual member's voice usually carries as much weight as the pastor's.
   b. The small congregation of 35 to 90 has standing committees and follows a congregational pattern in its decision making. This church expects the pastor to be more of an initiator, but most of the power is still vested in the congregation.
   c. The government of the mid-size congregation of 85 to 150 is representative rather than a pure democracy. This church expects the pastor to be an initiating leader and administrator.[1]

Most small-church people don't like top-down management. They are grassroots people, preferring that ideas come from the bottom up. So does this mean the pastor's ideas are those least able to get a fair hearing? No, it just means the pastor must find a bottom-up way to introduce those ideas.

If your church responds better to a bottom-up process, avoid presenting your idea first at a board meeting or in front of the congregation—both top-down approaches. Instead, why not plant your idea informally with several key people? Throw it out between innings at a ball game, or mention it over coffee at the cafe. Then sit back and listen. If the idea doesn't pop up anywhere, it probably means people didn't like it. You've just been spared trying something that wouldn't have flown anyway.

But if people like the idea, it will come up at a board meeting or congregational meeting, usually with the person presenting it claiming ownership. When the idea is proposed in this bottom-up way, you can be pretty sure it will fly—which is far more important than your getting credit for it.

Step 3: Be patient. Don't be in a hurry. Your ideas don't have to be implemented today. Your church has gotten along for many years without your ideas. And remember, there are few causes worth dying for—dying professionally, that is. It's far better to let your idea die and for you to live to see another day of pastoral ministry in your church.

Vision in the Small Church

Vision has become something of a buzzword among church leaders. We've recently seen the ministry vision of a few entrepreneurial pastors lead to phenomenal numerical growth in their congregations. In the small church, though, all this talk of vision can seem as out of place as Robert's Rules of Order at the family dinner table. I (John) discovered some of the reasons for this when Valley Chapel went through the process of formulating a ministry vision statement.

One reason is limited resources. A week before we finished work on our vision statement, our Sunday school superintendent and financial secretary both resigned. The Sunday school superintendent was relocating to another community, and the financial secretary had started a new job that made it impossible for her to continue. Suddenly our grand design for the next century didn't seem all that important. I was more concerned about getting through the next quarter.

Another reason the small church feels less need to define a vision is its family orientation. At the beginning of Valley Chapel's vision formulation process, I outlined the project to one of our members. Her face fell as she listened.

"If you expected me to say I liked the idea," she said, "I'm afraid I can't." I was surprised and disappointed. I had considered her one of our more progressive members.

She went on to explain. "As a teacher, I see this sort of thing all the time. It always turns out to be some administrator's idea of what we teachers should be doing." At the core of her lack of enthusiasm was a fear that by focusing on the vision, we would lose sight of the needs of our own people, and our church would lose its family quality.

The pastor may have more of an outward focus while the congregation's focus is primarily inward. The pastor often anticipates a field of ministry much broader than the congregation does, partially because most members view the church as a place to be served rather than as a place to serve or as a base for outreach.

The pastor in most cases has moved to town specifically to minister to the community and naturally sees the community as a mission field. But most of the church's members have a different perspective. To them the community isn't a mission field; it's home.

The small church may be ambivalent about growth. Pastors usually focus on the positive consequences of numerical growth—a greater potential for ministry, an increased financial base, and a larger presence in the community. They sometimes forget that numerical growth is also painful for the congregation.

As the church moves from one stage to another in its growth, it experiences a kind of death and rebirth. Its structure changes. The atmosphere changes. People experience more distance from both the pastor and the rest of the members. Even in the most successful transition, the church experiences real losses and must go through a period of disorientation and grief.

Tension between a future- and a past-orientation is also common. Unlike the large church where vision normally takes the form of long-range plans for outreach and growth, the vision of the small church often comes from its past. The small church is proud of its history and much of what it does is designed to preserve that heritage. What does the small congregation hope the future will be like? For the most part, just like the past.

While inwardly focused, short-term thinking is understandable, it is also dangerous because it can limit the church to a maintenance ministry. Effective pastoral leaders will be responsive to their congregations' felt needs and address them, while at the same time helping them develop a vision for ministry that looks outward and toward the future.

The small congregation does not need to feel obligated to become a megachurch, but it does have a responsibility to evangelize. This is not because bigger is better, but because the church is heir to Christ's calling to "seek and to save what was lost." Evangelism is essential to every church's mission regardless of size.

Faithfulness to our calling does not guarantee that the church will grow, but growing the church is not our job. It's our job to share the Good News through word and action and to create an environment that welcomes newcomers. It is up to God to actually bring growth: "I planted . . . Apollos watered it, but God made it grow" (1 Cor. 3:6).

George Barna recommends that a church's vision statement be limited to a short paragraph and satisfy three requirements: (1) it must identify the kind of people to whom the church has been called to minister; (2) it must describe what the church hopes to accomplish through its ministry to this target group; and (3) it should identify the distinctives of the church that define its particular ministry niche.[2]

At Valley Chapel our vision-formulating process was guided by three questions: Who are we? Where do we live? What is God calling us to do? Asking these three questions helped us learn several valuable things about our church and our mission.

Through conducting interviews with people in the community, we realized we could not afford to wait for the unchurched to come seeking us. We would have to go to them. To reach them, we would have to try to think more like missionaries and less like consumers. We would have to reach out to them in ways that take into account the fact that they see their primary needs as being relational rather than spiritual.

I've seen signs that a vision to reach outside ourselves has begun to take root. Not long after we finished crafting our vision statement and its goals, a member called me. A friend had told him of a used school bus our church could buy for one thousand dollars.

"John, it's in really good shape," he said excitedly. "My friend was going to buy it himself, but now he is planning to move."

I could hardly believe my ears. We hadn't expected to meet the goal of buying a vehicle for our Sunday school for another six years. The comment his wife made, however, excited me even more. "I thought the Lord would do something through these goals," she said, "but I never expected him to give me the burden I now have for this ministry."

Another couple in our church is hoping to rent a house in the country of Albania to use as a base for ministry during the winter months when they are not occupied with the demands of their farm. "If you had told me ten years ago I would be doing this," the wife says, "I never would have believed you." This is the same church where, nine years earlier when I mentioned to one of our key members that evangelism was going to be a high priority in my ministry, I was told, "We're not that kind of church."

Early in the twentieth century, the English explorer Sir Ernest Henry Shackleton placed an ad in a London newspaper that read: "Men wanted for hazardous journey: small wages, bitter cold, long months of complete darkness, constant danger. Safe return doubtful." Thousands responded to the challenge.

Does the challenge of leadership in the small-town church seem daunting? Good! We are starting off on the right foot when we realize that the task is bigger than we are. But God has called and is calling thousands of people to accept this challenge, and he has promised that we will not have to do it in our own strength. When we say yes to that challenge, we are embarking on the adventure of a lifetime.

9

Little Churches That Did

Many rural churches today are in towns that are shrinking, even dying. Others are in communities rapidly changing due to rurbanization. These changes, far from being welcome, may be perceived as threatening to the members of these congregations. They may feel like they are in danger of losing what has made their churches special through the years.

In light of these changes on the rural landscape in North America, is there really any reason to believe rural churches can have a bright future? We believe there is. Yes, the changes are real, and they pose real challenges. But, like Sam Walton, some pastors and congregations have looked at these same realities and seen potential where others could see none. Here are the stories of how four such churches found ways to tap into their untapped potential.

An Isolated Rural Church

Kingsburg (South Dakota) Church was located in a dying town where nothing was left except the church. In fact you could drive through town without knowing it. The church itself had declined steadily until it had only five families left. The building, erected in 1912, was run-down with a leaky roof, peeling paint, and an undependable furnace. There were no Sunday school rooms—only curtains dividing classes in a dingy, noisy basement. The people were discouraged.

Most folks would have said it was time to close the doors. But rather than closing its doors, the Kingsburg congregation called on Chuck and Pauline Myers to assume the leadership of its church. The congregation called the right people. Chuck and Pauline have the ability to see potential where most see none. They had devoted more than thirty years to helping declining rural congregations turn around.

Just before coming to Kingsburg, they had pastored in Oshoto, Wyoming, population two. At Oshoto, Chuck had drawn a circle with a ten mile radius around the town, then figured out how many people lived within that circle. There were 131, too few from which to build a church, most folks would say. But not Chuck and Pauline Myers. When they left Oshoto after four years, they left behind a self-sustaining church of seventy people—about half the community!

Similar turnarounds had taken place at the two churches the Myers had pastored prior to Oshoto. Now Chuck and Pauline were hoping to provide the leadership needed to breathe new life into another struggling church.

It wasn't long before folks in the surrounding area realized that something special was happening at Kingsburg Church. Chuck and Pauline worked tirelessly to offer encouragement to a church that was down and to reach out to the unchurched in the area. They focused their work in two areas.

Relationship building. Chuck sees himself as somewhat shy and withdrawn—a behind-the-desk administrator type. But, rather than say, "They'll just have to accept me the way I am," Chuck has deliberately worked at strengthening this aspect of his ministry.

Chuck and Pauline can be seen all over town. They immerse themselves in community activities. They are in people's homes and those same people are often in their home. They are always conducting several Bible studies—most of them outside the church building. And their church services are informal, warm, upbeat, and participative.

Ministry to children. Having six children of their own, the Myers recognize the value of a kid-friendly church. At Kingsburg they started a children's ministry, which quickly mushroomed to more than sixty children. On a personal level, Chuck and Pauline are always careful to give much attention to children, not ignoring them as they talk to adults. Years ago, Chuck found a way to draw funny faces that keeps kids tugging at his coattails, begging him to draw pictures for them.

God blessed the Myers's diligence. In particular, the people from nearby Springfield (population thirteen hundred) responded. It wasn't long before the people at Kingsburg Church realized they needed a different facility to meet in. Attendance had increased to nearly seventy on an average Sunday morning. Most of the folks in the church, including Chuck, were leaning toward building a new facility on their present site. But a more radical vision was emerging in Pauline's mind.

For nearly two years Pauline had been driving by a vacant dormitory building in Springfield, thinking, *This building would be ideal for our church.* She quietly prayed about the building, saying nothing to anyone but the Lord. Eventually, Pauline presented her idea to Chuck. At first, Chuck was skeptical. He thought relocating might create division in the church. After all, the church had been in its present location for a long while; the building was full of history. But when the idea of relocating to the neighboring town was presented to the congregation, not a single person opposed it.

They began negotiating with the owners of the dormitory. For months it seemed hopeless. They were far apart in price. So the Myers and their congregation devoted themselves to fervent prayer. They knew if God was in it he could make the impossible happen.

Finally, after nearly a year of negotiation, the Kingsburg congregation acquired title to a seventy-one-hundred-square-foot building plus a four-thousand-square-foot basement and five acres of land for fifty-four thousand dollars. To build the same facility would have cost over three hundred thousand dollars. The church praised the Lord for this wonderful provision, but that is not the end of the story. Fifty-four thousand dollars may not sound like a lot of money, but for the Kingsburg congregation, it seemed like an impossible sum to raise. This farming community had just gone through several years of drought, and before the drought years there were the farm crisis years of the early 1980s. Even without building payments, the church was already stretching its pocketbook to meet its regular operating expenses. How would it ever find money for the building?

Getting the building for a song was already God's provision; now the church looked to God once again to provide the funds. God did not let them down. The congregation rallied, giving sacrificially. Folks from miles away heard what was happening in Springfield and sent generous donations. Many of the Myers's friends gave. Several large contributions came in.

Paying for the building was just the first step. Next, the dormitory had to be converted into a church. The Kingsburg people went to work. Hundreds of hours were put into cleaning and remodeling. Chuck worked right alongside the rest of them. He quietly spent 160 hours applying 40 gallons of paint. This inspired the congregation to sacrifice their time as well.

On the day when the first service was held in the new building, the doors of the old church were locked, and the congregation proceeded to its new meeting place in a caravan.

Through the whole building transition process, Chuck was very careful to make clear that getting into a building was not an end in itself, but a means to an end. He had seen far too many churches whose sole vision was to acquire a facility. Once they were in their new building, they would comfortably settle back into a maintenance mode. Knowing this danger, Chuck selected as the theme for the dedication, "We are pressing on," emphasizing that the Kingsburg Church's vision had only begun.

Two years after purchasing the building, on the Sunday before the final payment for the building was due, the church still needed another twenty-one hundred dollars. An offering was taken, and the ushers immediately went to count the total, while the congregation waited in anticipation. Finally, the ushers brought the report to Pastor Myers. Dramatically he leaned over the pulpit and announced, "Folks, this building is paid for!"

A Traditional Rural Church

One of my (Ron's) favorite places to preach is in John's former church. Green Valley, Illinois, a traditional rural town of seven hundred people, is hardly the kind of place you would expect to find a thriving church, but that's what Valley Chapel is.

Valley Chapel is a warm and affirming congregation. Enter on Sunday morning and you will be greeted by several people before you have a chance to sit down. The worship services exude warmth—a family feeling. This church laughs together a lot—a sign of a healthy church.

Valley Chapel has a simple but meaningful Sunday morning service that includes vibrant worship, blending traditional hymns with contemporary choruses sung from an overhead projector. The church is blessed with several musicians who not only play well, but play with energy and enthusiasm. The worship service also includes time for intimate sharing and praying. An elder usually leads this part of the service, asking the congregation for praises and requests. The people pray passionately. In fact congregational prayer is the engine that drives this church. John notes, "Every major ministry thrust has been accompanied by an emphasis on the importance of prayer."

The church has a strong leadership team. It is clear that these leaders were not chosen hastily or just to fill empty slots. In fact just recently the elder board was expanded by two because the church had matured to the point where two more members were qualified and ready to serve.

John credits his leaders with being committed to personal growth and faithful to their calling. They are always stretching and challenging the church, not afraid to include an element of risk in the process. They are not afraid of change, but are the real change agents in the church. Their flexibility sets the tone for the congregation.

Valley Chapel has strong local and global outreaches. I am particularly impressed with this church's local evangelism. In many small towns I hear the church folk say that their community is saturated with the gospel, so there is no need to evangelize. That's not Valley Chapel's attitude. It actively and strategically evangelizes in its community. It shows movies on Main Street, sponsors concerts in the park, hosts Valentine's banquets, and puts on one of the best vacation Bible schools around.

At the same time, the church is growing in its commitment to foreign missions. Two years ago when it began its missions program, the missions committee decided to give priority to supporting organizations that emphasize church planting to unreached people. It also decided to encourage church members to participate in short-term missions opportunities as a way to help develop a missions-minded church.

The missions committee was excited when the church doubled its first year's faith promise goal, then watched in amazement as one-third of the church's members got involved in short-term missions the following year. Suddenly Valley Chapel's impact was no longer confined to the small community of Green Valley, but stretched from Illinois to North Dakota to the former Soviet Union. David VanOrman, a farmer who has made four mission trips—two to Mexico, two to Albania— is typical of those who have been involved in the church's short-term ministry when he says: "I didn't want to grow old and wonder why I didn't go when I was younger. I want to use every opportunity the Lord gives me to make a difference."

When John first came to Green Valley, the congregation met in a small storefront with no rest rooms. When he left nine years later, they were worshiping in an attractive and practical facility.

Last, but not least, Valley Chapel has a healthy self-image. What a contrast to the many small churches that are down on themselves! Positive preaching has helped. "I was struck by a remark Fred Smith made in *Leadership* about giving the congregation permission to succeed," says John. "It helped me see that much of the focus in my preaching was too negative. I was so busy pointing out what they weren't that the people had a hard time seeing what they were or could be. I began to affirm the church for their successes. Changing focus had a positive effect. It's been a long time since I have heard someone say, 'We're just a small church.'"

A "Wal-Mart" Church

A Wal-Mart church is a hub church drawing from several communities.

In the mid 1930s five farmers met to pray under an old oak tree near the one-room schoolhouse that served the settlement of New Castle, Illinois. These godly men, deeply concerned about the spiritual needs of their community, prayed for a church to be established. Today the settlement is gone, but the church they prayed into existence is thriving on that very spot.

Some may wonder why New Castle Bible Church should be included in this honor roll of "little churches that did." Most who pastor small churches would hardly consider a congregation of nearly three hundred to be small. But when Phil Somers began his ministry at New Castle more than ten years ago, the church's attendance seemed stalled at 150, with decline a real possibility. Today New Castle has grown to be a multistaff church with double services. This kind of growth is even more remarkable when you consider that this is a country church nestled between the small communities of Deer Creek (population seven hundred) and Mackinaw (population fourteen hundred).

Though others might have seen New Castle's location as a handicap, Phil saw it as an asset. Rural towns tend to be competitive and are occasionally hostile to neighboring towns; residents who do not attend church in their own community are more likely to make the extra drive to the city than to attend worship at a nearby rival town. Because New Castle is halfway between Deer Creek and Mackinaw, it has escaped being exclusively identified with either community. Its ability to draw from both towns plus other nearby communities has proven that New Castle is actually in a strategic location.

The effectiveness of New Castle's ministry can be seen in a number of growing ministries that serve the congregation, the community, and the church at large. In addition to strong youth and Sunday school programs, the church is developing ministries focused on retirees, young couples, and women. Its missions program has been energized by an emphasis on personal involvement in short-term ministries. New Castle has also developed a conference ministry, hosting a yearly prophecy conference and two half-day seminars that focus on the spiritual development of men and women.

Several key factors have contributed to New Castle's success. First, they have an emphasis on people and their mission statement captures this:

> New Castle's purpose is people . . . to lead them to Christ and love them . . . to pray for them and praise the Lord with them . . . to reach out through ministry here and missions everywhere . . . to apply God's Word and advance our spiritual gifts . . . to strive for excellence in service as we await the Savior.

Both Phil Somers and his assistant, Dennis Schlappi, are deeply involved in the lives of the congregation; neither could be described as a "desk jockey." Phil comments, "I love to meet the farmers in their fields or the businessmen in their workplaces and pray with them." Dennis focuses his attention on the young people of the church and explains: "My students trust my teaching and know I care about them as individuals. Those are important elements in a ministry with youth."

While success might provide Phil and Dennis with opportunities to step up to a larger church, neither is interested in upward mobility. They are committed to each other as a pastoral team and to a long-term relationship with the church. "I can't imagine myself pastoring any other church," Phil explains. "There is no other place I want to be." This kind of commitment has led to continuity and stability in New Castle's ministry. Phil and Dennis have worked together for nine years and the church's secretary has been there for more than ten.

For the past several years Phil has been stretching his own leadership skills by fine tuning his philosophy of ministry and working on a personal mission statement. He describes his personal ministry vision this way: "I dream of planting and mothering another church in a place nearby where there is no gospel witness; of seeing our congregation as both reaching out to the lost and in towards each other effectively." He also hopes to see the church staff expanded with both full-time and part-time personnel drawn from the church family and some of the church's own people commissioned for full-time ministry at home and abroad.

Phil attributes New Castle's success to the power of God, the responsiveness of the congregation, and leaders within the congregation who understand the importance of prayer.

New Castle Bible Church meets in an attractive building that looks as if it should grace a postcard or church bulletin cover. Money and effort have been invested to expand the facility, make it more comfortable, and develop the landscaping. While church facilities have been de-emphasized in some ministry circles, the church building is still important to rural residents. A dilapidated and unattractive building can be a barrier to attracting new members. While the building isn't the church, a facility that allows for future growth and is both comfortable and attractive can be a tremendous asset.

Nearly a half century after the farmers' prayer meeting, a memorial stone was placed beneath the old oak tree that shaded the five farmers as they prayed. The inscription reads: "On this spot more than fifty years ago godly men met to pray asking God to plant a thriving church and God has answered their prayer." When Phil contacted the stone carver about making the inscription, the craftsman warned that it would take a special kind of stone to create a monument that would last for centuries. In a way, New Castle Bible Church is itself that kind of monument: a memorial to God's grace and the fervent prayers of godly people, a monument made of living stones, built on the foundation of Christ himself.

A Rurban Church

Recognizing that their community was no longer a traditional rural setting, the founders of the Community Bible Fellowship Church (CBFC) of Red Hill, Pennsylvania (population: eighteen hundred), determined from the outset that their church would be a student of their surroundings and seek to meet the challenges of the times in which they lived. CBFC started three years ago with a small core group of 35 to 40 people, but they have grown rapidly to an attendance of between 150 and 200 today.

CBFC is one of the most creative churches we have seen. Their creativity grows out of careful analysis of their community. For example, the church recently began an Adult Christian Education (ACE) program. Because of the diverse and busy schedules of their members, ACE is offered at several times each week so members can choose which one to attend. And, recognizing the "shopping mall" mentality of their culture, an attractive, contemporary-looking brochure lists the various ACE electives that are offered, so almost anyone can find something of interest. While some classes are held at the church, several of the electives are taught in homes.

The church has an hour-and-a-half worship service of which the first half is lively and appealing to children. At "half time" the children are dismissed to go to what most would call Sunday school classes, which run concurrently with the sermon for the adults. So teachers won't miss the sermons, they all receive tapes of the messages.

Why this unconventional approach? Pastor Ron Denlinger and his leaders knew their human resources were limited, not just because the church was small, but also because of the busy lifestyle of the rurban person. Knowing they did not have enough children's workers to run both a Sunday school and a children's church, they decided to combine them.

For the same reason, CBFC has analyzed every program the church offers. Rather than diving into all kinds of ministries, they have carefully thought through what they will offer, making sure it is top quality, but not overly demanding of workers' time. They try to offer one solid program each week for each age segment of their congregation—one for children (Sunday school during the worship service), one for adults (ACE), and another for teenagers on Wednesday evening. In between, special events—banquets, vacation Bible school, fellowship gatherings—are scheduled to meet special needs.

CBFC is also not afraid to take risks. More than once they have attempted the "impossible." As a result, God has worked. God has worked because this church deliberately creates opportunities for God to work. Why would anyone want to attend a church where God is not working? How can God work if the church does not create opportunities that call for the supernatural? Ron Denlinger observes, "There is an enthusiastic spirit within this group rooted in a sense of awe that God is moving among us."

One example of looking to God to do the impossible occurred when the church purchased a building. They had their eye on a building, which they frequently brought before the Lord in prayer. The asking price was $750,000, far more than it would have been wise for such a small congregation to pay.

The church offered $237,500, but their offer was rejected. Then came the word: "The property is going to the auction block."

On the Friday before the auction, they held a special prayer meeting from 7:00 P.M. to midnight. Auction day came, and when the gavel fell, the building was the church's for $165,750— nearly $72,000 less than it had offered for it. Ron says, "Our greatest thrill is not that God gave us a *building*. The real thrill is that *God* gave us a building."

Another "secret" is that this congregation cares not only for the needs of the body, but also for the needs of people in the community. They know they can't meet all the needs of the community, but they can meet some.

In this area, instead of accommodating their culture as they did with the ACE program, they recognize the need to be counter-cultural. The church knows that boomers and busters tend to be isolated and self-sufficient, thinking they can handle their own needs, so they don't involve others in their needs. For example, when boomers go on vacation, they don't ask their neighbors to take care of their pets; they take them to kennels. When they need to have something repaired, they don't ask friends for help; they hire someone to do it. When they're sick, they don't tell anyone.

CBFC wanted to create an environment that ran counter to these cultural trends. They found various ways to do this. When a mother needed some time to get her life in order, three families in the congregation took in her children. A sixteen-year-old was killed in a shooting at the local high school shortly after Ron preached a message about off-loading stress through prayer. The church decided to put feet on that sermon. It quickly called a prayer meeting and put an announcement on the local Christian radio station. Ron didn't expect many to come, but more than sixty people prayed together that night, twenty of them high schoolers, and Channel 6 News from Philadelphia was there to cover it. They introduced the story by saying that the "community was coming together to deal with the tragedy, and the first place they came together was in church."

These churches are not alone. Their examples could be multiplied many times over throughout North America. They and others like them show that, no matter what the setting and circumstances, the small church is big enough to accomplish great things for God. Every day churches just like yours are touching people's lives with God's transforming love.

Epilogue

Imagine...

A small-town church that does not question its significance, because statistics are not its focus. Rather, it emphasizes strengthening and building the lives of people, leaving the statistics to God.

A small-town church whose pastor has overcome the temptation to use the small church as a stepping stone to "bigger and better" things.

A small-town church that celebrates its intimacy while enthusiastically welcoming newcomers into that intimacy.

A small-town church that responds to the challenge of limited resources by becoming radically creative. Instead of despairing about the obstacles it faces, it steps out in bold faith, expecting God to do something entirely new.

A small-town church that, in fresh and creative ways, builds its ministries around the people it has, rather than trying to fill slots created years ago.

A small-town church that does not try to imitate larger churches, but studies itself and its community, then prayerfully designs ministries uniquely suited for its place and time.

A small-town church whose members actively share their faith in their own community.

A small-town church that continually sends its people to various places around the globe in obedience to the Great Commission.

A small-town church whose pastor is filled with compassion for people in the church and community, a pastor who appreciates the church's strengths and is patient with its weaknesses, a pastor who feels, "This is truly home, and these people are my family."

Whatever your church's size, location, or circumstances, this, we believe, is what your church has the potential to be. With God's guidance, inspiration, provision, and power, your church can develop its untapped potential. It can become all God has in mind for it to be.

Notes

Chapter 1: *Five Myths of Ministry Success*

1. Kennon Callahan, *Effective Church Leadership: Building on the Twelve Keys* (San Francisco: Harper and Row, 1990), 4.

2. Ken Vetters, "Evangelism in a Small Town," *Leadership* (Spring 1994), 74–78.

3. Francis Schaeffer, *A Christian View of Spirituality* (Westchester, Ill.: Crossway, 1982), 9.

4. David Roper, *A Burden Shared* (Grand Rapids: Discovery House, 1991), 12–13.

Chapter 2: *In Search of Greener Pastorates*

1. Kent and Barbara Hughes, *Liberating Ministry from the Success Syndrome* (Wheaton: Tyndale House, 1987).

2. Eugene Peterson, *Under the Unpredictable Plant* (Grand Rapids: Eerdmans, 1992), 28–29.

Chapter 4: *The New Rurban Frontier*

1. The name of the pastor and church have been changed to protect the church's privacy.

2. *Residents of Farms and Rural Areas* (U.S. Department of Commerce, Bureau of the Census, October 1990), 1.

3. Stephen McMullin, "In the Pastoral Pastorate," *Leadership* (summer 1987), 74.

4. Ibid., 73.

5. 1980–1989.

6. *Residents of Farms and Rural Areas*, 1–3.

7. Janet Bodnar and Kevin McManus, "Kissing the Big City Goodby," *Changing Times* (August 1990), 28.

8. Marnie Mead Oberle, "Author's Cat Connections Extend Far," *Peoria Journal Star*, 6 August 1991, D12.

9. William Dunn and Andrea Stone, "Seniors Pose a Challenge for Towns," *U.S.A. Today*, 5 April 1991, A1.

10. Arnold Hamilton, "Golden Acres," *Dallas Morning News*, 13 May 1990, A28.

11. Andres Duany and Elizabeth Plater-Zyberk, "The Second Coming of the American Small Town," *The Wilson Quarterly* (The Woodrow Wilson International Center for Scholars, winter 1992), 21–22.

12. One of the criteria Norman Crampton used to select the most appealing small towns in his book, *The 100 Best Small Towns in America* (New York: Prentice Hall, 1993), was how many conveniences of a city were either present in the town or nearby.

13. We first read the word *rurban* in an article by James Berkley titled "What I Learned about Rurban Ministry," *Leadership* (winter 1982), 72.

14. Carl S. Dudley and Douglas Alan Walrath, *Developing Your Small Church's Potential* (Valley Forge, Pa.: Judson Press, 1988), 43–44.

15. Findings reported in two articles: Lee Mitgang, "Country Kids No Better Off," *Peoria Journal Star*, 23 May 1990, A1, 3; Dean Olsen, "Rural Teens at Risk," *Peoria Journal Star*, 3 June 1990, D1. The General Accounting Office has reached similar conclusions according to Cheryl Tevis, "Rural Drug Abuse Is Serious," *Successful Farming* (January 1991), 64.

16. Linda Swanson and Larni T. Dacquel, "The Effect of Economic Stress on Family Structure," report for the USDA Agriculture Outlook Conference released 2 December 1992.

Chapter 5: *Adjust or Bust*

1. Paul Hiebert, "Culture and Cross-Cultural Differences," *Perspectives on the World Christian Movement* (Pasadena: William Carey Library, 1981), 374.

Chapter 6: *Use Your Two I's*

1. Laurence Wagley in his book, *Preaching with the Small Congregation* (Nashville: Abingdon Press, 1989), uses the phrase "participatory preaching" to describe some of these same concepts we are encouraging.

2. Warren Wiersbe, *Real Worship* (Nashville: Oliver Nelson, 1986), 172.

3. Ibid., 172–73.

Chapter 7: *The Great Niche Hunt*

1. George Barna, *User Friendly Churches* (Ventura, Calif.: Regal, 1991), 51.

2. Lyle Schaller, *The Small Church Is Different* (Nashville: Abingdon Press, 1982), 129.

3. Sam Walton, *Sam Walton: Made in America—My Story* (New York: Doubleday, 1992), 109–10.

4. Most of the suggestions were gleaned from chapter 12 of *Made in America*, though some came from other parts of the book.

5. Much of this summary of Walton's book was inspired by an article written by Gary E. Farley, "How to Become a Thirty-Mile Church," *The Baptist Program* (November 1992), 10–12.

Chapter 8: *Secrets of Small-Church Leadership*

1. Schaller, *The Small Church Is Different*, 161–63.

2. George Barna, *Without a Vision the People Perish* (Glendale, Calif.: Barna Research Group, 1991), 130.

Ron Klassen is general director of the Rural Home Missionary Association, which plants and strengthens churches in small towns. He received the master of theology degree from Dallas Theological Seminary and pastored small churches for several years. He is the author of many articles, a conference speaker, a seminar leader, and an adjunct Bible college professor. Ron, his wife, Roxy, and their three children live in Illinois.

John Koessler is assistant professor of pastoral studies at Moody Bible Institute. He received the master of divinity degree from Biblical Theological Seminary and the doctor of ministry degree from Trinity International University. He has pastored a small church and works as a freelance writer, contributing articles to Christian periodicals. John, his wife, Jane, and two sons live in Chicago.

The authors may be contacted as follows:

Ron Klassen
Rural Home Missionary Association
P.O. Box 300
Morton, IL 61550
309-263-2350

John Koessler
Moody Bible Institute
820 N. LaSalle
Chicago, IL 60610
312-329-4000